Always In Style
with *Color Me Beautiful*

Your Shape, Your Style!

*How
not to
look older*

see page 98

Always In Style

with
Color Me Beautiful

Doris Pooser

foreword by
Carole Jackson

ACROPOLIS BOOKS LTD.
WASHINGTON, D.C.

ACROPOLIS BOOKS, LTD.
Colortone Building, 2400 17th St., N.W.,
Washington, D.C. 20009

Printed in the United States of America by
COLORTONE PRESS
Creative Graphics, Inc.
Washington, D.C. 20009

Attention: Schools and Corporations
ACROPOLIS books are available at quantity discounts with bulk purchase for educational, business, or sales promotional use. For information, please write to: SPECIAL SALES DEPARTMENT, ACROPOLIS BOOKS LTD., 2400 17th ST., N.W., WASHINGTON, D.C. 20009

**Are there Acropolis Books you want
but cannot find in your local stores?**
You can get any Acropolis book title in print. Simply send title and retail price, plus $1.50 cents per copy to cover mailing and handling costs for each book desired. District of Columbia residents add applicable sales tax. Enclose check or money order only, no cash please, to:
ACROPOLIS BOOKS LTD., 2400 17th St., N.W.,
WASHINGTON, D.C. 20009.

Always In Style with Color Me Beautiful was designed by Robert Hickey; Chris Borges, Assistant Art Director; Tom Smoak & Mary Kay Carter, Artists.

All models appearing in *Always In Style with Color Me Beautiful* were photographed by Jerry Mesmer, Adams Studio, Washington, D.C.

Styling by Janet Leigh Hume   Art Direction by Robert Hickey

A special thanks to Valerie Avedon (*Summer/Autumn*), and Laurie Dustman Tag (*Summer/Winter*) for appearing in *Always In Style with Color Me Beautiful*.

All other models in *Always In Style with Color Me Beautiful* appear by arrangement with The Erickson Agency, McLean, Virginia.

Patricia Buchholz (*Winter/Autumn*)   Carol Ann Pettit (*Spring/Winter*)
Joan Clark (*Winter/Spring*)   Sharon George (*Spring/Autumn*)
Susan Allenback (*Winter/Summer*)   Jennifer Van Horn (*Autumn/Spring*)
Lori Estep (*Summer/Spring*)   Phyllis Pritcher (*Autumn/Summer*)
Holly O'Dell (*Spring/Summer*)   Jeannie Kincer (*Autumn/Winter*)

Cover Photo by Jerry Mesmer.
Cover photo makeup and styling by Janet Leigh Hume.
Fashion illustrations by Brenda Burkholder
Body and clothing diagrams by Christine Turner

Library of Congress Cataloging-in-Publication Data

Pooser, Doris,
    Always In Style with Color Me Beautiful.

    1. Beauty, Personal.   2. Clothing and dress.
3. Color in clothing.   4. Color of man.   I. Title.
RA778.P73   1985   646'.34   85-15613
ISBN 0-87491-785-9

ACKNOWLEDGMENTS

The following people have contributed to making this book possible. A special thanks to each of them.

Sandy Trupp, Valerie Avedon, Robert Hickey, Dan Wallace, Chris Borges, John Hackl, Irma Gallagher, and Al Hackl from Acropolis Books Ltd. for their excellent work and for giving far beyond their responsibilities.

Phyllis Avedon, my editor, for her talent and contributions.

Carole Jackson for giving me an opportunity to share my knowledge.

Philomena Hughes for her efficiency, support, and management skills.

Lisa Ramsey for her professional input.

Rebecca Giles for her assistance, endless wit, and enthusiasm.

Frances Wronski for teaching me more about style than I ever realized.

Lastly, to the three most important people in my life: my two sons, Todd and Jeff, for their patience, enthusiasm, and support, and to my husband, Jim, for his encouragement, dedication, and love, which made it all possible.

FOREWORD

Doris Pooser was born with a flair for fashion! Her love and enthusiasm for design and style are infectious, and I admit that Doris has converted me to the point where my enthusiasm for fashion is equal to my enthusiasm for color. Like so many women, I was intimidated by "fashion." Doris's energetic approach to personal style, plus her insights on body lines, fashion lines, and individual body shapes makes fashion understandable, and, best of all, *fun.*

I know that you, too, will thoroughly enjoy expanding from the original Clothing Personality categories presented in *Color Me Beautiful* into the new dimensions presented in *Always in Style with Color Me Beautiful.* Doris's approach is revolutionary, and you will be brimming with confidence in making just the right choices for yourself, no matter what fashions are "in."

Doris and I have immensely enjoyed working together on expanding the seasonal color theory. It was important when I wrote *Color Me Beautiful* to present the basics in a simple and understandable way. But now it's time to take poetic license and expand your colors, too. Doris has developed a clever and scientific way to add colors to your palette based on the subtleties of your skintone, hair, and eye colors. While some people do fit perfectly into one color category, others really need extra colors to take full advantage of their coloring. And some people simply want the excitement of adding more colors to their life! They want to know how to make a fashion statement through color without detracting from their best look. It's all here for you in this wonderful new book.

Doris Pooser has been an important member of the Color Me Beautiful family for some time, as the International Trainer for our Color and Image Consultants in the Far East and Australia. Her talent for organization is unsurpassed, and she is a delightful, giving person as well. Best of all, when you have read *Always in Style with Color Me Beautiful* you will be able to apply her discoveries to yourself and enjoy your own new adventure into style and color.

With love,

Carole Jackson

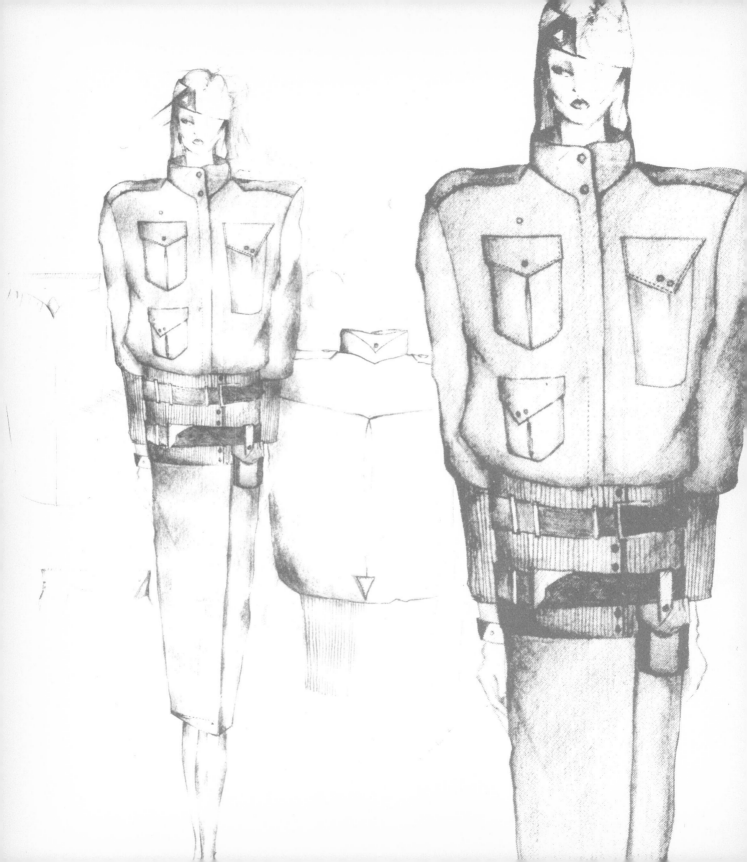

CONTENTS

If Only...

"If only!" How many of you have an "if only" list? Mine was *long*. If only I were shorter, if only I didn't have such long arms and legs, if only my complexion were better, if only my face didn't happen to be so square, or if only I could look like my friend Mary.

I didn't just *say* "if only." I tried to *change* me. I frosted my hair to get rid of the red, contoured my jawline with dark foundation to make my face look oval, slouched to make myself look shorter, and spent years embarrassed about my complexion. I even tried to dress like my friend Mary. I tried to wear the silk blouses with soft bows that looked so wonderful on her. The harder I tried, the more frustrated I became. It's hard work trying to be something you're not—trying to look like someone else and knowing that it's impossible.

I finally decided to take a good look at myself, accept myself, and start over. I analyzed my body size and shape and compared it with others. I noticed the characteristics of clothing that complemented all of the different body types. After testing my observations on hundreds of others, I realized that each woman has her own individual style, which is determined by her unique body size and shape, her facial shape, her coloring, and finally her personality. You don't need to try to change any of these things. You *do* need to identify your unique characteristics and work with them.

I now accept and emphasize my square jawline, wear clothing that balances my long arms and legs, take advantage of my height, wear makeup and color's that complement my coloring, and save a fortune at the hairdressers, since I no longer change my hair color. *It is so much easier and so much more fun being me.* I also receive far more compliments. I now have my own individual style; it's very different from Mary's. I can enjoy her look without envying it because I now enjoy mine.

And that's what this book is all about: showing you how you can develop your own truly individual style.

Doris Pooser

Doris Pooser

PART I

STYLE

What is a Well-Dressed Woman?

Designer Coco Chanel first dressed her elegant clientele in suits in the 1930's. When Hollywood beckoned, her influence spread far beyond the couturier world. On screen and off, women began wearing suits. The "Chanel suit," which evolved during the fifties, has since become a classic.

The skirt is straight and elegantly simple. The short, collarless jacket has a straight, edge-to-edge closing. The simplicity and versatility of her design have made it internationally popular—available in all price ranges, in all colors and fabrics. To be "well-dressed" has often been simply a matter of wearing a Chanel suit.

And then there's the basic black dress, with a plain jewel or scoop neckline, a straight skirt and fitted waist, and long or short sleeves, depending on the season. The little black dress has been a tradition for generations. It has also been a social necessity—essential to own, regardless of how you looked in it. You were always "well-dressed" in your basic black.

Our casual lives have also been strongly influenced by the fashion industry. A case in point: the seen-everywhere "alligator" shirt made famous by tennis star Rene LaCoste. Although it has spawned look-alikes bearing polo players, horses, and foxes, many men—and women—continue to rely on the alligator shirt to keep them safely well-dressed on the sports scene.

The corporate woman of the seventies was expected to emulate her male counterparts—navy pin stripes, tailored blouses, and minimal makeup were the well-dressed business woman's uniform of the day.

Today, however, women are less willing to conform, either to the expectations of the corporate world or to the dictates of the designers.

A matter of balance

Today's well-dressed woman thinks in terms of the total picture she creates. This includes her makeup, clothing, and the way she carries herself. To fully express who she is, the colors, designs, fabrics, and details involved must all balance with her coloring, her body size and shape, and her facial features. These factors must also balance with who she is internally, which is reflected in the way she moves and walks. This non-verbal message, which comprises 55 percent of what she says to others about herself, is essential to her style.

This all-important balance is created when what you are wearing looks like a natural extension of you by complementing your characteristics as well as your personality. How can we accomplish this? Few of us, especially since we grew up with the security of "dictated" styles, were ever taught what to look for when selecting our clothing. Instead, we learned to shop sales, or to buy what looked nice on our friends. Consequently we never succeeded in defining our individual style, let along relating it to the clothes we should wear.

Some lucky souls can put on an article of clothing and instinctively know that it creates the balance and harmony that make it right for them. The styles they choose always seem "theirs," and they have a knack for mixing pieces and accessories to create interesting, exciting looks. They're the ones envied for their natural flair for fashion.

Many of those on today's best-dressed lists are there because they have this innate ability to select the right clothing. Others make these lists because they can afford personal shoppers or have found one or two designers whose clothing consistently works for them. Although these women are fortunate in that they have been able to develop their style, they too can benefit from understanding why the clothes they wear work so well for them. It is always fascinating and exciting to learn the "whys," and to learn to perfect what you already know.

But those of use who have not been blessed with a natural flair for style—who have not yet managed to reach best-dressed status—*can* acquire the skills that it takes to get there. The list is less important than the satisfaction of knowing that you qualify. When you as an individual reach your maximum potential—when you always look as wonderful as you can—it will be because you have discovered your individual style and how to put it to work for you.

Every one of us wants to look good, to feel good about ourselves, to look youthful and up-to-date. Whether we shop in Paris or buy our clothes in our local department store or boutique, we can all look fabulous. How? By knowing what to look for when we select our clothes.

Beginning the Search for Style

Dramatic, Classic, Elegant, Chic, or Just You?

Today's designers offer us a bewildering array of styles from which to choose. With so many options, deciding on the ones that are best for us can be a real problem.

Many recent books have defined categories of styles to help those struggling to find their own special look. Carole Jackson, author of the best-selling *Color Me Beautiful*, classifies styles as Dramatic, Classic, Natural, and Romantic. In *Dressing To Win*, Robert Pante categorizes women as Glamorous, Elegant, Spicy, and Chic. These categories are ideal starting points. That have helped make us aware of the differences in styles and encouraged us to search for that one special, perfect style. I spent years believing that when I finally arrived at a specific style and classification, it would answer all of my questions and meet all of my needs. I analyzed each of the different categories, hoping to find the one that ideally suited me.

I have always felt classic and formal, preferring clothing with a traditional cut. Yet the classic Chanel jacket, pin-striped suit, and shirtwaist dress made me feel and look out-of-proportion—awkward and rather ordinary. This was an incredibly frustrating aspect of searching for my style since it can be such an elegant look on the right person. But even though the traditional classic styles didn't seem to work for my body size and shape, I was determined not to give up the search for my own classic look.

Many people have called my style Natural because I like texture and wear it well. Yet I have never been comfortable in informal clothes and rarely, if ever, go without my makeup, even on my day off. I look better in a plaid or tweed jacket than in an all-plaid suit, which is too heavy and bulky for me. My facial features and bone structure cannot take the weightiness of a tartan plaid or a stacked-heel walking shoe. More importantly, I do not enjoy a Natural's informal lifestyle.

I have also been called Romantic. I love movement and softness in my clothing and have a long willowy body that allows me to wear clingy fabrics. However, I am not comfortable in glitter, flounces, laces, or chiffon. I prefer tailored styles, even for my dressy looks.

I have often had the desire to be Dramatic. I am tall and fairly slender, but do not have dramatic coloring or strong, exotic features. I love to follow the latest fashion trends and enjoy trying new fashion looks. Even though I felt it would be fun and exciting to wear certain exaggerated styles, in the past I lacked the confidence to try them. I was never sure where "high fashion" ended and "trendy" began!

Robert Pante, in one of his "salons," described me as elegant and glamorous. Was that because of the way I dressed, carried myself, and moved, or was it because of the role in which he saw me that day? Doesn't everyone want to feel glamorous at some time during their life? I must admit that I don't feel terribly glamorous sitting at my typewriter at 10:00 at night, but I do still have my makeup on. Perhaps I am glamorous at heart.

The more I studied the different categories of styles, the more I realized that none of them really described *me*. In addition, coming from a generation that tended to have seasonal styles dictated to them, I really wanted more flexibility than they seemed to offer. I also wanted to know how to wear *more* than one style.

Our lifestyles today make it important for us to be able to wear many different styles, depending on the occasion, not to mention our moods and our need for excitement and change. By expanding the definitions of the categories, we can end the search for a single style and consider several. Let's stop for a moment to look at these expanded definitions.

A **Dramatic** person is often described as tall and slim, with vivid coloring, angular features, and a certain sophistication. Does that mean that someone who's five-foot-two can't look dramatic?

Absolutely not! It all depends on how you define "dramatic." I have always considered dramatic to be a high-fashion look that anyone can wear, regardless of her size and shape, if she truly has the desire for this look and understands the rules of dressing. Many petite women look marvelous in ultra high-fashion clothes. Actress Susan Lucci, who has appeared in leading fashion magazines, graces the popular soap opera "All My Children" with a fabulous dramatic look. Diminutive Susan always looks wonderful in her dramatic clothes.

Many tall, slim, angular women just don't look right in a high-fashion look and would never feel comfortable dressed that way. The off-stage Carol Burnett is a perfect example. She is obviously comfortable in conservative clothing, and has given priority to her desires, feelings, and personality in selecting clothing. When dramatic is defined as an extreme in line and design, we realize that very few people are able to dress in a dramatic style while looking and feeling appropriate for all occasions. Cher is one of the few who can wear extremes and obviously feel comfortable in them. Bob Mackie, who designs clothing for both Carol Burnett and Cher, has been able to create styles that are appropriate for both by considering their physical characteristics and personalities as well as their likes and dislikes.

In the study of style, extremes are rarely considered good fashion. Let's define Dramatic, then, as a high-fashion look that is tastefully done and can be worn by anyone, regardless of her size and shape, once she understands what to look for when selecting her individual clothing styles. Because this look is not appropriate for all occasions, it's important to expand your knowledge of styles so that you know where and when a particular style can be used effectively.

A **Classic** is often thought of as being of medium height with even, well-balanced features; someone who is well-proportioned and has a relatively conservative outlook on life. But what about the person who is well-balanced, well-proportioned, of medium height, who *isn't* conservative, or at least is conservative only part of the time? She should not be limited by a particular style in which she is not really comfortable. And those of us who are not necessarily well-proportioned, and who are taller or shorter than average, sometimes want or need a classic conservative look.

Today's corporate woman has made great strides away from her conventional "uniform." Women in the business world now feel freer to dress in ways that express their individuality. Career achievements can mean even greater flexibility in clothing choices, but a conservative air remains important; her flair for fashion should never overshadow a woman's professional skills. Surveys confirm that certain colors and looks promote her credibility and enhance the power look. Her status as an equal among men dressed in conservative business suits is improved when she wears a suit or jacketed dress. Navy blue, brown, camel, and gray increase credibility and should therefore be an integral part of a corporate wardrobe. There have been significant changes in recent years, but it is still necessary and wise to dress conservatively in a corporate setting.

My definition of Classic, therefore, is a conservative look that everyone has a need for, depending on the occasion. Some people are naturally more conservative than others, and will want to use this look more often. Each of us, however, regardless of size and shape, should have her own version of the Classic look.

Does **Romantic** mean ruffles, glitter, and high-heeled shoes? Yes, at times. But everyone can have her own romantic look if we think of Romantic as an outfit and mood for a quiet evening at home with a special someone. Each of us would wear something different to achieve a personal romantic mood. Jane Fonda, Nancy Reagan, and Joan Collins would each dress differently, translating "romantic" according to her individual style. Joan Collins might wear a black charmeuse dressing gown trimmed in black lace. Jane Fonda might choose a silk smoking jacket with a shawl collar and silk trousers. Nancy Reagan might don an elegant ivory caftan with a mandarin collar. Romantic means different looks to different women. Some like glitter and heels, and love being "dressed up." These perennial romantics may have to work at not looking overdressed in their daily lives.

The word **Natural** conjures up thoughts of someone tall, with a sturdy or athletic build, who is casual and enjoys informality. Yet many people are born with large bones and sturdy builds but feel very formal and conservative. (Or they like to be dressed up all the time, or are mad about the dramatic look.) As we've pointed out, body size and shape alone should never dictate style. Everyone likes a casual, informal look at certain times. Most working women appreciate the opportunity to escape from the need to get "dressed" in the morning, or to have to apply their usual makeup. But those who tend to rely on the casual look (and whose lifestyles suit this way of dressing) must be wary of the times and places when they need a more professional or business look.

In classifying styles, it is important to realize that we are describing many things. The words dramatic, classic, natural, and romantic evoke thoughts of occasions, moods, and personalities as well as overall impressions of types of clothing that would be appropriate for these times and places. Unfortunately, these "overall impressions" are not sufficient.

One of my colleagues once commented that she was analyzed as a Summer, a Classic, and Spicy. She sent out a plea to her friends to help her find a Summer's blue, soft Classic, Spicy dress. Using this description would not only complicate the search, it would produce a wide range of dresses, depending on who did the choosing.

As you can see, these kinds of labels do not give us specific information about actual pieces of clothing and how they should relate to us personally. They can, however, be used effectively for describing times, places, and personalities. There are times and places for all looks and it is necessary to know when to wear each of the styles. The appropriateness of dressing for the occasion cannot be overemphasized. The Appropriate Occasions chart explains some of the times and places for wearing different styles.

Appropriate Occasions for each Style

	Dramatic	*Classic*	*Natural*	*Romantic*
Work	Entertainment	Corporations	Teachers	Not Appropriate
	Fashion Industry	Law, Medicine	Child Care Workers	
	Department Store Buyers	Politics	Work involving physical labor	
	Boutique Owners	Government Employees	Work not dealing with public	
	Art-related Industries	Social Workers	Service-oriented professions	
	Interior Designers	Teachers	Grocery and variety store personnel	
	Advertising	Real Estate		
	Media-related professions	Politicians		
	Public Relations dealing with above			
Casual/ Leisure Time	Sports events	Church functions	Sports events	Candlelight dinner
	Picnics	School meetings	Picnics	Evening at home
	Shopping	Civic events	Recreational activities	
	Recreational activities	Board meetings	Shopping	
	Relaxing	Political gatherings	Gardening	
			Relaxing	

Chart continues on next page.

	Dramatic	Classic	Natural	Romantic
Social and Obligatory Events	Cocktail parties	Cocktail parties	Resorts	Cocktail parties
	Dinner parties	Dinner parties	Vacation areas	Dinner parties
	Movies	Theatre—only when dressy top, jewelry, shoes, and bags are added to conservative suits and work clothing	Family-style restaurants	Dances
	Weddings			Theatre
	Lectures, if group is young and related to one of the above work areas			Weddings
				Formal occasions
		Funerals		
		Lectures		
		Speeches		
		Presentations		

Note: Those who are self-employed have considerable flexibility in determining what is appropriate. The deciding factor should be their audience and/or the people they will be dealing with. To dress 'appropriately' means that you will look successful and credible, but will not intimidate or make others feel uncomfortable.

Knowing who you are

Once you've established your guidelines for appropriateness, it's important to consider your likes and dislikes and your personality. Each of you, because of who you are, will tend to be most comfortable with one or two styles. This is fine when the occasion offers a choice. You must, however, learn to appreciate the need for different looks. As you gain confidence in understanding how your clothing relates to you, you will be surprised at your new interest in different types of clothes. You will then be able to dress in a manner that fully describes who you are as a person.

No matter how precisely a style is defined it still doesn't tell us what to look for when selecting clothing to be worn on a specific figure. Classifications are interesting, fun, and informative, but in order to use them to develop your individual style, you must first understand what they mean with respect to your individual physical characteristics. It is important, therefore, to learn some basic rules about the construction of your clothing and how it relates to your figure's requirements. When you have these parameters within which to work, you can learn to dress in exactly what is right for you.

Before I learned the guidelines and how to relate clothing construction to my body, I spent many a sleepless night worrying about what I would wear for that special event. I can remember piles of discarded outfits on my bedroom chair as I frantically searched for the one that looked right. I hate to admit it but I have had days and evenings ruined because I didn't feel right in the outfit I finally selected and didn't know why. Now that I have a practical and easy set of guidelines to tell me what to look for in selecting my clothing, I always feel good about the way I look and have the time and energy to devote to more important matters.

In order to define and determine your own individual style, it is important to look at your physical characteristics. You were born with a particular body type and special facial features. When you find the appropriate clothes to complement all of your positive characteristics you can reach and stretch in the style direction that makes you feel most comfortable. Once you understand your physical characteristics you will be able to develop your style and flair by combining the line, designs, fabrics, scale, and colors that complement your special qualities. You can then create wonderful and unique combinations that reflect your personality and creativity.

Style: A Definition

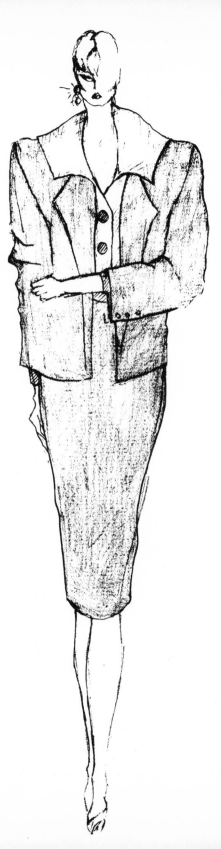

Which characteristics of clothing determine its style? Let's consider three parameters—line, scale, and color—and how each of these directly relates to your physical characteristics. Keep in mind that your clothing should be in balance and harmony with your body size and shape and your facial features. It should look as though it belongs on you, and is a natural extension of you. The line of your clothing—the silhouette line—should complement the line of your body. The amount of texture and any patterns you wear should be in direct proportion to this line. The scale of your clothing should be proportionate to your body size. And, of course, the colors you wear should complement your natural coloring.

As I take you step by step through line, scale, and color, you will learn how to analyze yourself to determine exactly what to look for when shopping for clothes. You must be honest with yourself and be able to look at yourself objectively. You were born with a special body size and shape as well as special facial features. You may wish you were shorter, taller, thinner, or whatever, but wishful thinking has no place here. You must accept yourself; accept what you have been given and make it work for you. You'll discover your limitations (everyone has them), but you will learn to work *around* them to play up your positives. You'll learn to turn the things you once thought of as faults into assets. You'll also find a new joy in being you as you reach to create exciting new looks that you never dreamed of before.

Q. *I have always been described as a Classic. I am well-proportioned, have an average build, and am shy. I am ready for a change. How can I change my look for the better?*

A. A classic tends to be conservative or to prefer a conservative way of dressing. You are obviously ready to be less conservative. When you find your correct body line and scale, you will be able to wear many different styles, depending on your mood and the occasion. As you gain confidence with your new look you will be able to reach for many variations. You do not have to start with an extreme; reach slowly in your new fashion direction. Try a new length skirt, a new big top or jacket. If you like it and are comfortable, reach a little further. Use your new guidelines to help you break out of your ultra-conservative style.

Q. *I have been told that I am a Natural. But I'm not athletic and feel very romantic and soft inside. How can I be me inside and out and still look right? What is my right style?*

A. No one needs to be limited to a single style of dressing. Look again at your physical characteristics as well as your personality and lifestyle. Once you truly understand your best lines, fabrics, designs, and colors, you will be able to develop your own distinctive style.

Discovering Your Body Line

Let's begin by describing line as it relates to you as an individual. When determining the best style to complement a particular body we need to analyze which body characteristics can be related to the corresponding characteristics of a piece of clothing.

Your physical characteristics are tangible and readily identifiable. How do you describe your body? Your facial features? Words like tall, short, thin, wide, broad, round, curved, or straight relate to a body type as *a type of line*.

A line is an infinite number of points with a direction. The direction can be straight or curved. Body silhouettes and facial shapes are often described as being diamond, square, rectangular, oval, pear, heart, round, or some combination of these. *Each of these shapes can be defined by either a straight or a curved line.* The diamond, triangle, square, and rectangle are created with straight lines. The oval, round, heart, and pear are created with curved lines.

The first step: analyzing the direction of the line of your body and of your facial shape and features. Will it be straight or curved? Your predominant overall characteristics—your body as well as your face—will be defined best by one of the following geometric figures: triangle, square, rectangle, ellipse, oval, or circle.

It is possible to see the silhouette of your body by looking at your shadow. Stand several feet from a solid, smooth wall. Face the wall and shine a light from behind you. Your shadow will be visible on the wall in front of you. Your silhouette line will be predominantly straight or curved. A predominant line can also be seen by looking at your body shape from a distance. Stand back and look at yourself in a full-length mirror. Some of you will see straightness, others will see curves. Some of you will find it difficult to identify the dominant line because suggestions of both straight and curved lines will appear. It is best to see your outline when looking at yourself in something like a leotard so that you see the silhouette of your body without being distracted by details.

Let's look first at those body shapes that have predominantly straight lines. These body types are often tall and thin, with small, flat hips, broad shoulders, small busts, and very few curves. Others in this category, though not especially tall or thin, have flat hips, square shoulders, and square or rectangular bodies. Remember, weight is not a factor here. We are looking at the silhouette line, not at height or weight.

If you find it difficult to determine your body line, look at your facial shape. The initial line impression that we get when looking at someone is often determined by their facial shape and features. "Straight" facial features are angular. A long slender nose, high cheekbones, a square or pointed jawline, and diamond or rectangular face shapes tend to create straight lines. Some straight lines on body types and facial shapes appear very sharp and straight, almost extreme; others are straight but less exaggerated. The sharper lines are best described by diamond and triangular shapes, the straight by square and rectangular shapes. In each case the body line and facial line can be described by

Straight-line body types

Look carefully at the examples of straight-line body types:

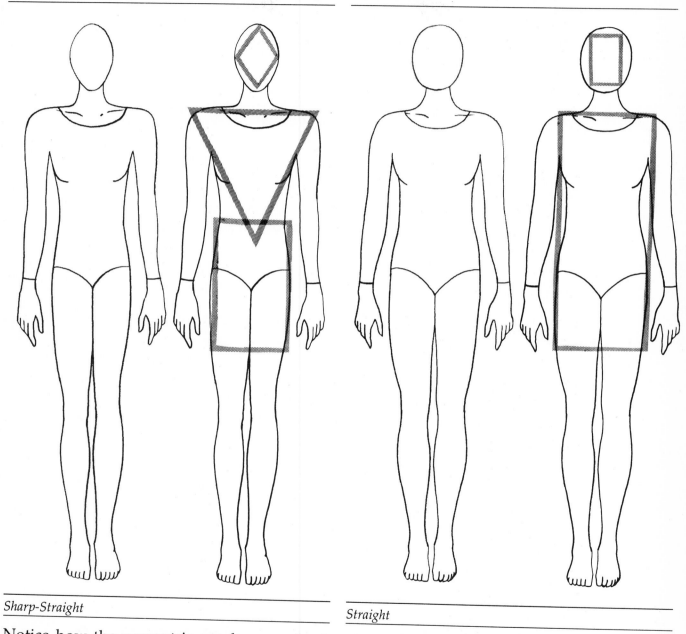

Sharp-Straight

Straight

Notice how the geometric overlays emphasize the basic shape of each body.

a straight line. One is a "sharp-straight" line; the other is a "straight" line. Do not let one prominent characteristic, such as a full bust, or large hips or thighs, distract you. Focus on the overall impact of facial features and silhouette line.

Those of you who have curved body-lines will have either soft smooth curves or obviously rounded curves. Your body silhouettes will appear rounded, with curved hips, shaped waists, and full busts.

Your facial shape will be oval, round, heart, or pear. You may have rounded cheeks, full lips, and round or almond-shaped eyes. These body shapes can also be described as round, oval, heart, or pear. In each case, the curved line can generally be described as oval or circle, depending on the degree of curve.

Rounded body types

Look carefully at the examples of rounded body types:

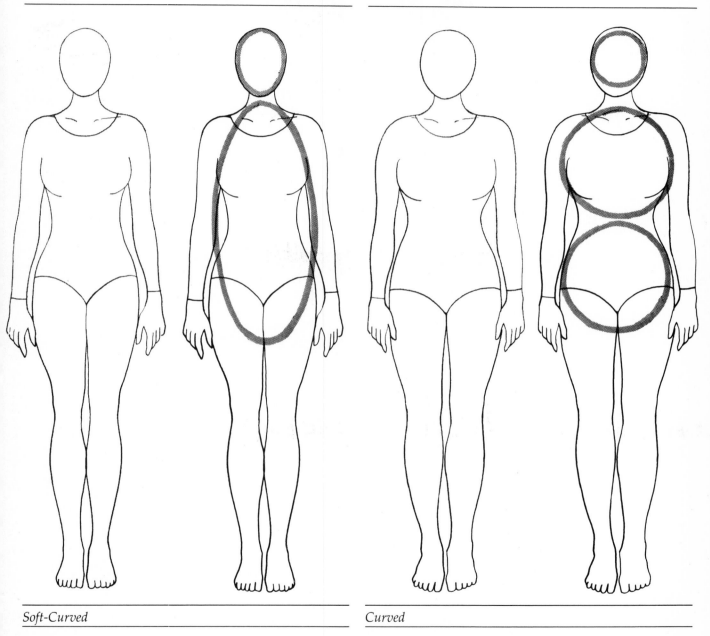

Soft-Curved

Curved

Notice how the geometric overlays emphasize the basic shape of each body.

If your "straightness" or curves are not obvious to you, your body line is probably best described as a combination of straight and curved lines. A tall person's body curves may not be readily apparent because her height accentuates the feeling of a straight line. The result is a softened straight line. You need not be tall, however, to have a soft-straight line.

The effect of a soft-straight line can also be seen in those whose facial "line" contrasts with their silhouette line. Curved facial features with a straight body, or a slightly curved body with straight facial features, combine to create the appearance of a soft-straight line. These straight facial features often have some softened edges that create a balance of straight and curved lines. The ellipse, or elongated oval, best describes this body type. If you are having difficulty determining your body line, you may well have a "soft-straight" body line.

Soft-straight body types

Look carefully at the examples of the two types of soft-straight bodies:

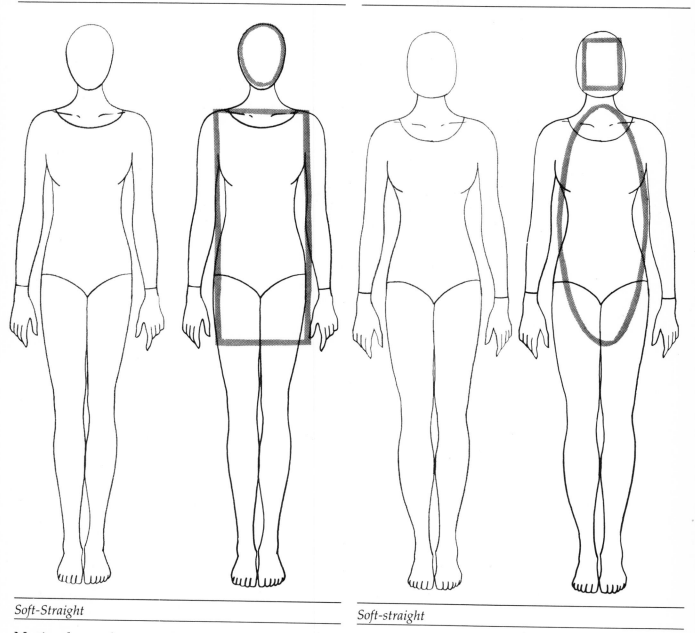

Soft-Straight

Soft-straight

Notice how the geometric overlays emphasize the basic shape of each body.

Q. *Whenever I borrow my roommate's blazer, I look older and feel stuffed into it, even though we wear the same size. Why?*

A. Blazers usually have straight lines, sharp lapels, and square details. You most likely need curved lines in your clothing. Look for shawl collars, slightly fitted waists, and curved details on your jacket. You can still achieve a wonderful classic look that will complement your body by wearing lines that are right for you.

Q. *I always admire lovely silk flowers pinned to a lapel or tucked behind an ear for evening. Every time I try this look, I feel ridiculous, like an aging Carmen Miranda.*

A. You most likely have angular features and straight lines to your body. Clothing and accessories with straight lines will look more balanced for you. Try a wonderful geometric pin on your lapel or a silk scarf with an abstract design tucked into your pocket.

Whether you are tall or short, slim or heavy, you will be able to describe your facial shape and body silhouette in terms of line, either straight or curved. It doesn't matter how straight or how curved, it's the overall impression that counts.

Look at these body figures, lined up from the straightest to the most curved. See the gradual movement from one body type to the next? Remember, there are many variations in between, since everyone has a unique and different body shape.

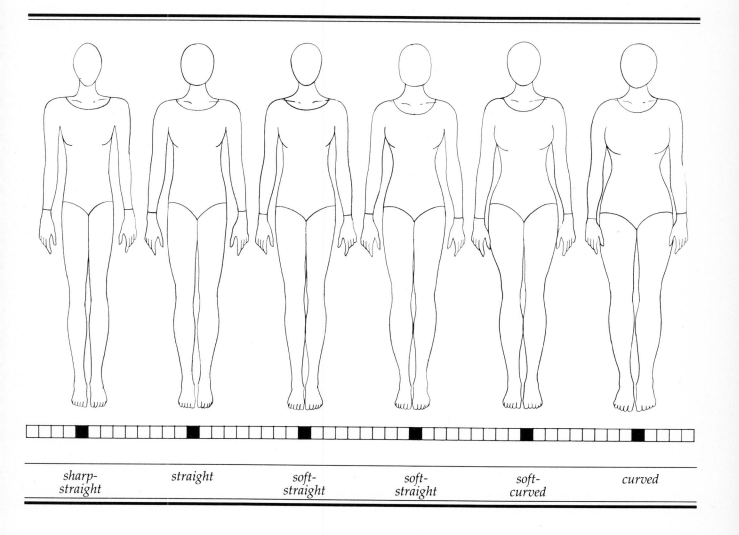

| sharp-straight | straight | soft-straight | soft-straight | soft-curved | curved |

The Geometric Categories chart describes facial and body shapes in terms of lines and geometric figures:

Geometric Categories

	Sharp-Straight	*Straight*	*Soft-Straight*
Face Shape	diamond square triangle	square rectangle oval (with square jaw)	oval ellipse
Body Shape	inverted triangle (broad shoulders) rectangle or some combination with the triangle	square rectangle	rectangle with slight curve
Overall	triangle (broad shoulders) angular face, straight body	rectangle	ellipse with the slight beginning of a curve
Figure with Overlay			

Geometric Categories

	Soft-Straight II	*Soft-Curved*	*Curved*
Face Shape	square soft edges on square or rectangle	oval round	round oval
Body Shape	ellipse	ellipse oval	oval or round
Overall	ellipse, slightly rounded curved	oval and defined curve	round, very curved voluptuous body
Figure with Overlay			

Where Do You Belong on the Graph?

If you are still having difficulty determining what your exact facial and body lines are, don't worry. We are simply looking for the predominant line that best describes the first impression of your physical characteristics. There is a continuous, gradual transition from the sharpest and straightest line to the softest and most curved. As individuals, each of us has a different and unique body line that can be classified somewhere from sharp-straight to curved, depending on the predominant line we project. There's no need to select an exact point on the line graph or become overly concerned about whether your body is sharp-straight or just straight. It is enough to know that you're in the straight range instead of the curved or vice-versa. You'll note that facial-shape and body-shape categories overlap in the charts of geometric shapes.

It's interesting to get a small group of people together and line them up in order, from the one who has the straightest silhouette and facial shape to the one who has the most curved. You will see a number of subtle variations. Even though several of you may have straight body lines, each will look different. Some lines will be sharper than others and some will probably fit into the soft-straight range. The purpose of lining up is to show the continuum of different body types.

For our purposes you need only find the *range* that describes your body size and shape. Elizabeth Taylor would be at **Range C**, Nancy Reagan would be at **Range B**, and Cher would be at **Range A**.

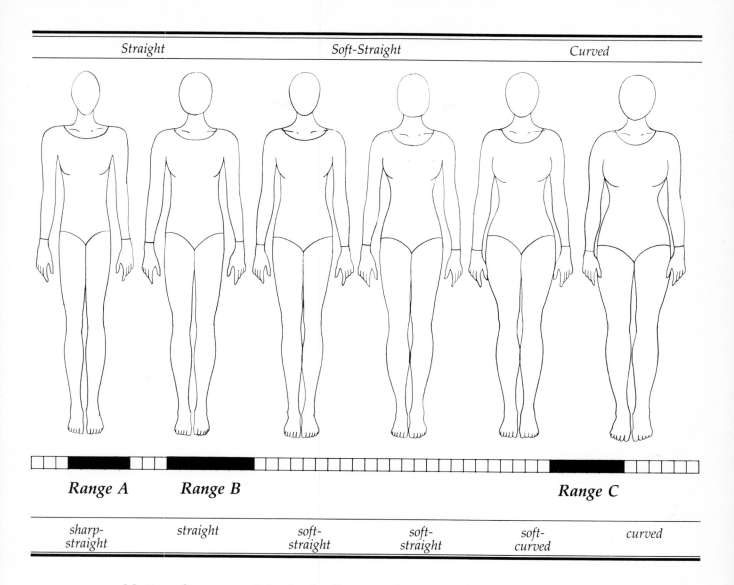

Straight	Soft-Straight	Curved

Range A　　**Range B**　　　　　　　　　　　**Range C**

sharp-straight	straight	soft-straight	soft-straight	soft-curved	curved

Notice that a straight body line can be very sharp and straight or lean toward soft-straight; the body line would still be defined as "straight." Soft-straight body lines may lean toward either straight or curved but will be considered "soft-straight." Both soft-curved and curved body lines may be considered "curved" for the sake of simplicity. We are therefore considering three basic types of body lines; straight, soft-straight, and curved.

Consider the following examples of well-known people with different body lines:

- **Sharp-Straight**

Cher	Nancy Kissinger
Pat Buckley	Diane Von Furstenberg

- **Straight**

Nancy Reagan	Geraldine Ferraro
Katharine Hepburn	Jacqueline Onassis

- **Soft-Straight**

Jane Fonda	Princess Diana
Linda Evans	Farrah Fawcett

- **Soft-Curved**

Ann Margret	Linda Carter
Jaclyn Smith	Joan Collins

- **Curved**

Elizabeth Taylor	Dolly Parton
Zsa Zsa Gabor	Beverly Sills

Some of you will have more flexibility in describing the line of your body because your characteristics are not extreme or exaggerated. Because the two extremes—sharp-straight and curved—are sharply defined, they are the easiest to identify. When the line is less well defined, the range is of course broader. But even those in the soft-straight range will see a **direction** of either straighter or more curved.

Degree of Flexibility

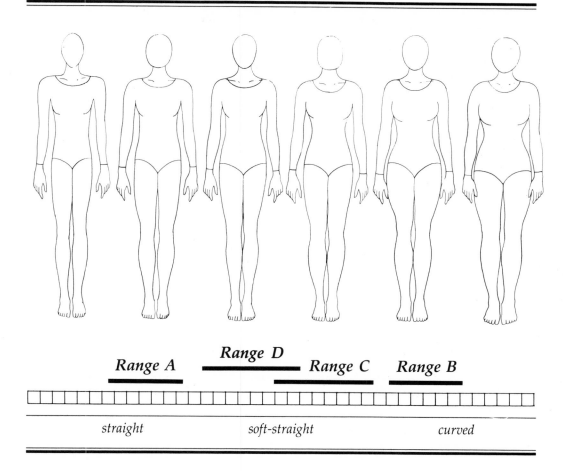

Range D

Range A   Range C   Range B

straight   soft-straight   curved

Line *range A* describes a body type with predominantly straight lines. It doesn't matter how straight; you simply fit in the straight range.

Range B describes a curved body. Regardless of the degree of curve, you can describe your range as curved.

Range C describes a soft-straight line which, because it is less well defined than either straight or curved, includes more body types. However, the direction of this range is toward curved.

Range D describes a soft-straight body whose direction is toward straight.

Moving along the continuum

As we leave our teenage years and move on through our twenties, thirties, and ensuing decades, we rarely retain the same body shapes. As we add weight to our frames, our body line tends to soften, as does our facial shape. Grace Kelly, as a young movie star, had soft-straight lines in her face and body. As she matured, Princess Grace of Monaco moved across the graph to a soft-curved line. Think back to your teens or twenties and you may notice a comparable progression for your body along the line graph. Although you may notice a movement from sharp-straight to straight, from soft-straight to soft-curved, or from soft-curved to curved, you will *not* see a movement from one end of the graph to the other. The bone structure and features you were born with, which are part of you, will always be present. Learn to recognize them and make them the foundation of your personal style.

Clothing as an Extension of You

Throughout history there has been enormous variation in the body line chosen as the personification of beauty. In the days of the ancient Egyptians, the tall, slender body and angular face were considered the ideal. Deities were always represented by these figures. During the development of western civilization, the curved, rounded body was held to be the height of beauty. The ultra thin has periodically been in vogue, as was the case during the "Twiggy" era. In today's fashion world the tall, slender, slightly curved body, with an oval face, is looked upon as the perfect combination.

Whatever body is "in," we are bombarded with information teaching us how to camouflage the bodies we have. When tall and thin is in we are told to cover the curves with straight lines. Straight and vertical lines do create length. A straight dress with a center seam does look longer than a dress with no seam. But how does it look on a curved body? It covers the curves, of course, but looks stiff and totally unrelated to the body beneath. There is an obvious separation between the clothing and the wearer; balance and harmony are missing. In order for clothing to be complementary, there must be a relationship between it and your body so that the clothing becomes a natural extension of you.

Imagine Elizabeth Taylor in a straight skirt and long, straight double-breasted jacket with sharp lapels. Why does this not present a balanced image? She needs clothing with soft curves to balance and complement the curves of her body. A soft wool crepe suit with a slightly flared or eased skirt, a short jacket with rounded lapels and slightly fitted waist would complement her figure. Cher, by contrast, would look wonderful in the straight skirt and jacket because it would complement her straight body shape and angular face.

Fortunately, today's woman has no need to change or camouflage her body whenever a new "ideal" emerges. She can instead work with her body line to emphasize its beauty. How much easier it is being ourselves, instead of trying frantically to change what we have. When we know we look our best we can enjoy being ourselves. And it is so much more comfortable!

The joy of being comfortable

I use the word "comfortable" frequently in my classes and lectures. In the movie *Same Time Next Year*, Alan Alda asks Ellen Burstyn to leave her husband for him. In spite of a long, less-than-perfect marriage, she declines. She says that her marriage is "comfortable." I often reflect on the meaning of comfortable as it was used in that movie and as it applies to our lives. Acceptance, security, satisfaction, belonging, and lack of pretense are all part of being comfortable. Being "comfortable" with our style is just one part of being comfortable with ourselves and our lives.

Too short to be "perfect"?

By working with your body lines when selecting clothing you will not emphasize over- (or under-) weight problems because you will be working with the right line, fabric, print, and texture for you. And accept your height. Why wear an unflattering dress so that you can seem an inch taller? Learn to wear the right lines and proportions to look fabulous and no one will think twice about your height.

So many articles have been written on how the short person can look taller. For example, she has been told to wear self-fabric belts to create a continuous line in her dress. I have almost never seen a self-fabric belt on a dress that didn't cheapen it. I prefer to add a contrasting leather belt or tie. Even if you are short, you can wear a contrasting belt lower on the waist, or wear hose and shoes the same color as your skirt hem to create a finished look. The positive addition of the wonderful belt will far outweight the potentially negative effect of wearing the wrong belt in order to look taller. If you are short, accept it. Don't spend your life wishing you were tall and trying to look just a little taller by wearing unflattering styles. There are too many wonderful looks for you to have fun with to bother trying to change your height.

Saying no to the ideal oval

Just as the "ideal" body has been promoted, so has the perfect oval face. We have been conditioned to strive for an oval face, and to make ours more so with the aid of makeup and hairstyles. How boring for everyone to be walking around with an "almost" oval face! An oval face is wonderful for the person who was born with it. The rest of us need to capitalize on the face shapes we have. Whatever the shape of your face, it helps make a statement of who you are. It is you. Play up the wonderful angles, emphasize the curves.

The most harmonious and most flattering clothing for your body will have the same line as your body and face shape. Don't try to change your shape — enhance it! Let's look at the clothing lines that will help you develop a successful personal style by working *with* your body line, not against it.

PART III

YOUR CLOTHING LINE

Which Clothing Line is Yours?

There are several lines to consider when looking at any item of clothing. One line is the silhouette line—the cut or exterior line of the garment. As with body lines, some articles of clothing have very sharp exterior lines and some have very curved lines, with all degrees of straightness and softness in between. Let's start with the sharpest, straightest clothing lines and go on to the most curved.

The sharp lines of the outfit in the illustration labeled *Sharp-Straight* are reflected in its strong angles; in the large, well-defined shoulders,

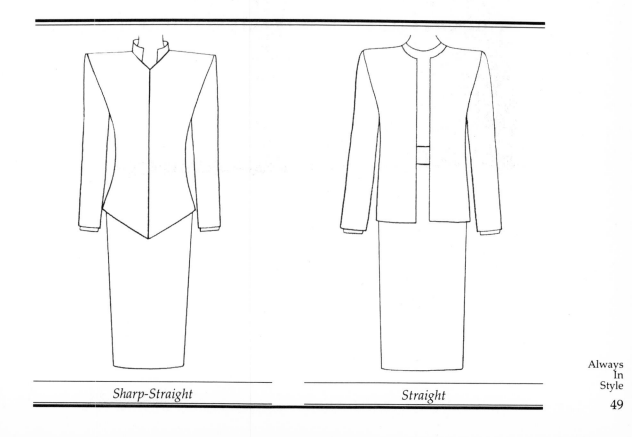

| *Sharp-Straight* | *Straight* |

closings, and hemlines as compared with the less exaggerated straight lines in the illustration labeled *Straight*.

Continuing across the spectrum we have what I refer to as the soft-straight-lined garment. A soft-straight line is achieved by using exterior construction lines that are smooth and soft with relatively little curve, or by using straight lines with a loose unconstructed fit and/or with a softly woven fabric. The looser construction provides a soft feeling without creating obvious curves. Here are two types of soft-straight-lined garments:

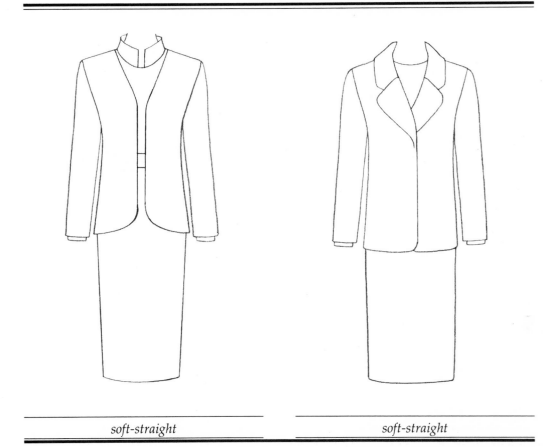

| *soft-straight* | *soft-straight* |

Next let's look at clothing with soft-curved and curved exterior lines. Notice the roundness and softness of the line. Curves are created by the garment's cut and shape, as shown in these figures:

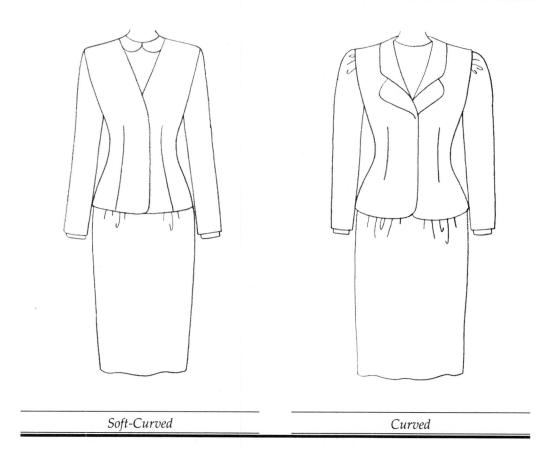

| *Soft-Curved* | *Curved* |

Types of clothing can be placed on a line graph in the same manner as different types of bodies. Thousands of types of silhouettes can be placed along the line. Keep the idea of a continuum in mind—not a limited number of individual categories.

It is the overall impression created by the outline, the flow, and the design of the garment that determines the predominant external line characteristics. You should be able to identify a general straight line, a curved line, or the in-between soft-straight line.

Continuum silhouette graph:

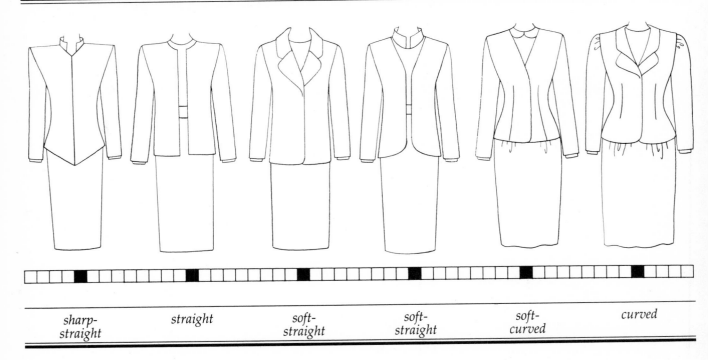

| sharp-straight | straight | soft-straight | soft-straight | soft-curved | curved |

Identifying Detail Lines

Detail lines emphasize and balance the total look of a piece of clothing. Many details can define a specific line. Those details that create a straight line should be used on clothing that has straight silhouette lines. Details that emphasize curves should be used with curved silhouettes.

For soft-straight silhouettes it is possible to use straight details as long as the overall impression of the finished piece has a soft flow to it. This can be achieved by use of a soft fabric or by using a single straight line in a garment when the remaining portion of the garment is soft in fit and line. An exaggerated straight line in the skirt can be offset by a cowl neck or shawl collar on the blouse. It is also possible to use some curved details, such as a round collar, yoke, or pocket, as long as the end result is not totally curved. An unconstructed jacket or straight pleated skirt will balance these curves. Overall, softened straight lines result from softened lines or a combination of straight and curved lines.

The details that best describe each line type are shown in the Detail Lines chart.

Detail Lines

	Straight Lines	Soft-Straight Lines	Curved Lines
Darts	long straight darts	straight or pleated	soft gathers instead of darts
	sharply defined or no darts		soft pleats instead of darts
			eased
Seams	well-defined seam lines	straight with unconstructed look	small seams
	top-stitching		curved seams
	contrasting piping, braid or trim	self top-stitching	no top-stitching
			fine top-stitching
			eased
Pleats	pressed down	pressed down with soft fabric	soft
	stitched down		unpressed
	asymmetrical	unpressed	gathered
			eased
Sleeves	set-in	set-in	gathered
	straight pleat at shoulder	raglan	eased
	square shoulder-pads	dolman	drop shoulder
	tapered sleeves	slightly padded shoulders	raglan
	crisp puff	rounded shoulder-pads	soft
			full and billowy
			rounded shoulder-pads

Detail Lines *(continued)*

	Straight Lines	Soft-Straight Lines	Curved Lines
Lapels	very sharp	notched with soft fabrics	rounded
	notched	shawl	curved
	straight with interfacing	sloping	shawl
	pointed	rounded	bias
	peaked	sharp or peaked with soft fabric	
Collars	pointed	straight with soft fabric	round
	notched	rolled	rolled
	straight with interfacing	cowl	cowl
	square	notched	notched with round edges
	stand-up		
	piped		
Pockets	well-defined	patch with rounded bottom	flap
	square	slash	rounded
	piped	flap	set-in
	slashed	square with soft fabric	
Jacket	edge-to-edge closing	self trim	slightly fitted
	square hemline	subtly defined waist	well-defined waist
	fitted or loose	loose	rounded bottom
	asymmetrical closing	unconstructed	curved closing
	contrasting buttons and trim		
Necklines	square	boat	round
	boat	curve	scoop
	jewel	turtle	draped
	contrasting trim	scoop	flounce
	V	V	ruffled
	mandarin	cowl	cowl

On the graph depicting detail lines related to the various clothing lines, notice the movement from one end to the other as the line gradually changes from straight to curved.

Detail Lines

| sharp-
straight | straight | soft-
straight | soft-
straight | soft-
curved | curved |

Now look at the graph that shows both body lines and clothing lines. Notice the direct relationship between the clothing line and the body lines. These clothes, by looking like a natural extension of these bodies, will create a beautiful balance.

| sharp-straight | straight | soft-straight | soft-straight | soft-curved | curved |

Body lines:

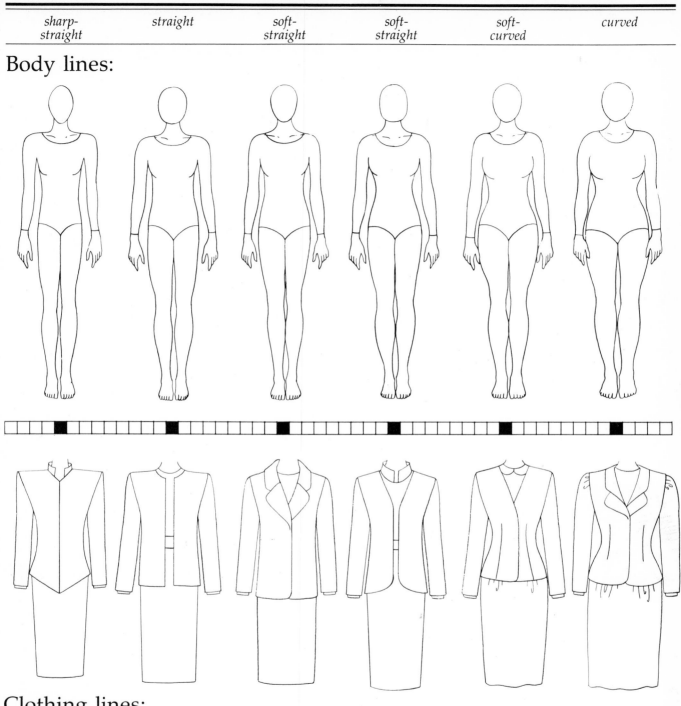

Clothing lines:

| sharp-straight | straight | soft-straight | soft-straight | soft-curved | curved |

Characteristics that Affect Clothing Lines

Fabric Weight

In looking at fabrics, it is important to consider weight, design, and texture, since they too affect the direction of the line. A line in geometry has only one dimension. But since we're using it as a fashion term, I am going to add other dimensions to help describe some of the characteristics of clothing and how they should balance with your special body characteristics.

Beyond the single dimension of a line—its length, including its direction—it is important to consider what I call the second dimension: the width of the line. When purchasing a pen, you have to decide what kind of point you want. Pen points range from fine to "standard" to broad. Consider the same jacket, drawn with both a fine-tipped pen and a broad-tipped one.

One looks lighter and finer; the other looks heavier and bulkier. What makes a garment seem to be defined by a fine line or a broad line, and who would wear each? This width must be considered for balance when we look at your bone size and your facial features.

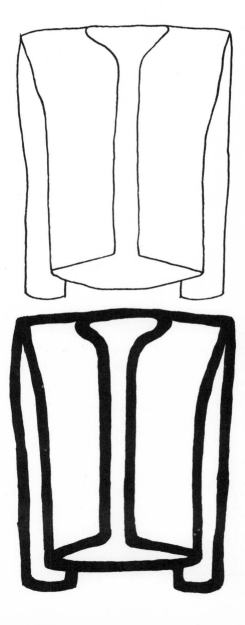

Some of you have fine, delicate facial features and are small-boned regardless of your weight. You need a fine line in the construction of your clothes to keep them from looking too heavy or bulky for your structure. How do we create a fine line in clothing? By using fine top-stitching, stitching close to the edge of the garment, or no top-stitching; fine, small buttons, trim, and details; and fine fabrics such as wool crepe, fine gabardine, fine broadcloth, silk, chiffon, boucles, and hand-kerchief linen. Whatever the fabric, it should not be bulky or heavy.

Some of you have bigger bones, and larger and stronger facial features. Larger bones give you larger wrists, ankles, legs, and so on. These are not faults or problems unless you make them stand out or exaggerate them by wearing clothes with too fine a line. The balance would then be lost and you would overpower your clothes. You need the jacket drawn with the broad-tipped pen. How do you create this feeling? With heavier top-stitching, saddle-stitching, and stitching that is double-spaced or a machine-foot away from the edge of the garment; heavier and larger buttons, accessories, and details; and fabric such as wool flannel, medium to heavy gabardine, tweeds, linens, raw silks, satins, knits, and similar fabrics. Avoid those that are light or delicate.

Those of you who have neither exceptionally fine features and small bones nor large bones and facial features will have greater flexibility in your fabric selection. Remember, however, you are looking for balance. Select fabrics that are neither too heavy nor too light for your frame. The traditional silks, cottons, wools, and linens come in all weights. The medium weight is best for you. Gabardine, challis, jerseys, and satins are all good choices in medium-weight fabrics. Be sure that your details, trim, and buttons are neither too small nor too large for a totally balanced look.

During President Kennedy's term of office, his wife Jacqueline made an enormous impact on the American public. Her classic suits and pillbox hats made a fashion statement that women everywhere wanted to emulate. Her style was correct for her body line. However, some of the fabrics she used were too fine for her bone structure and broad face-shape. Wool flannel or medium gabardine would have been more complementary to her stature than her choice of wool crepe. Heavy satin is a better choice for her Romantic look than gossamer chiffon.

To determine whether you have small, medium, or large bones and facial features, look at these charts:

Facial Features

	Fine	Average	Broad
Nose	Slender, narrow small, thin	*in between* *in between*	Broad, wide, flat strong, hook, large
Lips	well-defined, narrow small, thin	*in between* *in between*	full, round, large
Mouth	small, delicate	*in between*	large, full
Eyes	small, almond	*in between*	round, large, angular
Jawbone (from under ear to center of chin)	5"	5" to 6"	6" or more

Bone Size

	Wrist measurement	Ankle measurement
small bones	5½″ or less	8″ or less
medium	5½″ to 6″	8″ to 9″
large	6″ or more	9″ or more

Texture

Textured fabric may be described as rough, nubby, or loosely woven. It is the line's third "dimension"—its depth. The depth of the fabric affects the direction of the line as well as the width. Look at this picture of the same jacket shown with and without texture. Notice that the line is softened by the use of texture at the same time that bulk is added.

Examples of two jackets with and without texture.

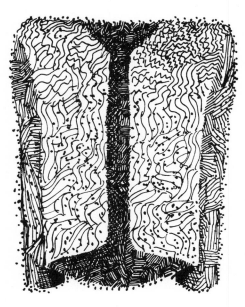
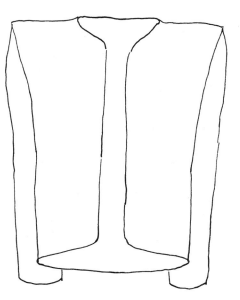

People often ask me, "Can everyone wear texture?" I tell them that this question has a number of different responses. Designers often relate texture to size and color. They frequently use more texture with muted and monochromatic colors to create interest. When we consider only color and size, we ignore the impact that texture has on line. It is important to think about how texture affects the direction of clothing lines.

It is very difficult to create sharp lines with a loose, nubby, or textured fabric. If you need a sharp line to your clothing to complement the straight line of your body, you should use little or no texture. Sharp-straight lines work best with tightly woven fabrics such as wool gabardine, sharkskin, or linen, or fabrics with a sheen, such as silk, charmeuse, and taffeta. The most texture that can be worn to effectively create a sharp line would be fine linen, Thai silk, or tightly woven twill or tweed. The use of stiff interfacing can help to achieve a sharp line with a fabric that would otherwise drape or fall softly, as can braid or trim.

Those of you whose bodies are in the curved category will find that texture does not work well. Texture will make your curves look bulky and bumpy instead of smooth and sleek, and will make you look overweight (the typical teddy-bear look). Soft, flat fabrics drape well and fall in the soft folds that are so necessary for a curved line. Fabrics such as silks, wool crepes, jerseys, challis, and wool and silk blends are all appropriate.

For those who need a soft-straight line, texture is wonderful. It was made to create the exact line you need. Any softly woven fabric with texture automatically falls into soft straight lines without creating curves. This does not mean that the person who needs soft-straight lines must wear only textured fabrics. She can wear all types of fabrics, including the smooth and shiny ones, as long as she uses the weight that corresponds to her bone size.

When you look at the graph, notice the use of texture with respect to the direction of the line. Those who need the soft-straight line can wear the most texture; less and less is used as you move out to the two extremes of sharp-straight and curved clothing.

Texture

Less◄----------------------Maximum----------------------►Less

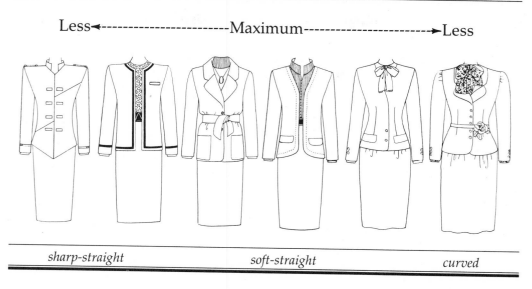

| sharp-straight | soft-straight | curved |

Print

The final relationship to line—the fourth "dimension"—is the print of the fabric. Prints, like texture, work best when used *with* the line of the garment rather than against it. From time to time designers assault our esthetic senses with prints that might best be described as vivid imagery. Bold cabbage roses and wild Hawaiian prints seem to emerge successfully every four or five years. They sell like hotcakes in the stores, but only for a season—as long as the fun fad lasts. Good style, by contrast, dictates that the line of the print be in tune with the line of the garment, thus creating an elegant and appropriate coordination.

The sharper and straighter your body line, the more geometric or "sharp" the print you wear should be. Soft floral prints used in sharply tailored styles do not create a balanced look. Those who need soft, curved lines are better in soft, rounded prints and watercolors. A rounded, soft feeling in the print as well as in the construction is essential to total balance. Those who can wear soft-straight lines need designs that are neither too straight nor too curved, and that allow for the movement and flexibility of the line. Here, too, they will have some flexibility in their selection of prints, since a geometric print will often be softened just enough by a soft-straight construction.

Notice the categories of prints, with respect to line:

- **Straight**

Geometric	Check
Stripe	Houndstooth
Abstract	Aztec patterns
Modern	
Sharp plaid	

- **Soft-Straight**

Paisley	Realistic
Stripe	Jungle
Plaid	Check
Animal motif	Tweed

- **Curved**

Floral	Paisley
Watercolor	Swirl
Realistic	Scroll
Rounded	

Taking exception

There are a few exceptions to note in terms of the relationship between print pattern and garment line. For example, if the line is strong and well-defined, the print pattern may vary a bit from the line. A small geometric print can often be incorporated into a soft-curved line. A stripe or plaid on the bias will be softened and will often work for a softer line. This combination may not be perfect, but is more acceptable than the reverse, a floral print made into a tailored style. The soft-straight line at times may combine a floral skirt with a straight jacket to create an overall impression of a softened line.

As a general rule, straight prints may be used in soft-straight or curved construction if, and only if, the construction is well-defined. Line and texture should be considered first; then print.

Twill Stripe

Stripe

Bouclé

Tweed

Tartan Plaid

Foulard

Linen

Floral

Houndstooth Plaid

Paisley

Houndstooth Check

The Lines
Designers
Use

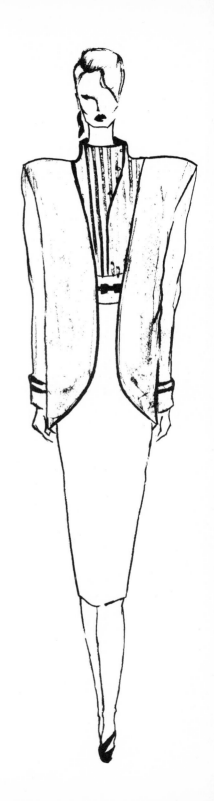

As I describe clothing and its "lines," details, construction, fabrication, and quality, I will use the work of some of the leading international fashion designers as examples. These designers set the trends for each season and provide a direction for all of us. Most use a specific line when creating their collections, which makes it possible for us to compare these lines as they relate to our body lines. Few of us can afford to buy these creations, just as few of us can afford a painting by Picasso or Monet. We can, however, learn a great deal from them as we become aware of what to look for with respect to line, quality, design, and scale. And even though these designers may be out of reach for you financially, NEVER pass up an opportunity to try on these designs—to familiarize yourself with the fit and feel of perfection. Observe designer collections in fashion magazines and in boutiques and department store displays. You will gain a reference point and a guide to help identify lines in more affordable price ranges.

The moderate-priced designers and manufacturers often use a favorite line, but are more likely to incorporate several different lines into their collections. They do this because they look to many of the major international designers for ideas and trends, and most importantly because they are appealing to a larger and more diversified market.

Here is a list of the major international designers with the lines they tend to use most frequently. I have also included the moderate-priced designers and manufacturers with the lines seen frequently in these collections. Remember, you will be able to find several lines in their collections, which makes it particularly important to begin to recognize the different body lines in clothing construction.

International Designers

- **Straight lines**
  Adolfo
  Chanel
  St. John
  Andre Laug
  Yves St. Laurent*
  Carolina Herrera

  Louis Feraud
  Castleberry
  Mary McFadden
  Gucci

- **Soft-Straight**
  Perry Ellis
  Calvin Klein
  Bill Blass
  Giorgio Armani
  Donna Karan

  Issey Miyake
  Yohji Yamamoto
  Escada
  Gianni Versace

- **Curved**
  Halston
  Zandra Rhodes
  Valentino*
  Emanuel Ungaro

  Oscar de la Renta*
  Betty Hansen
  Hanae Mori

*Often use extremes of both straight and curved lines

Moderate-Priced Designers and Manufacturers

- **Straight**

Geiger

Pendleton

Albert Nipon Sport

Jones of New York

J. G. Hook

Evan Picone

Stanley Blacker

Schrader Sport

Kasper for J. L. Sport

- **Soft-Straight**

Carol Little

Anne Klein II

Perry Ellis Porfolio

Geoffrey Beene Sport

Adrienne Vittadini

Liz Claiborne

Calvin Klein Classifications

Willie Wear

St. Tropez

Blassport

Anne Pinkerton

- **Curved**

Tahari

Norma Kamali

Christian Dior

Ellen Tracy

Prophecy

Flora Kung

Ralph Lauren

Cloak of Many Colors

Marc d'Alcy

Nancy, Jane, and Liz know their lines. Have you learned yours?

Nancy Reagan has straight-line body and facial features. She needs straight crisp lines in her clothing and can wear many of the straight-line designers' clothing well. Jane Fonda needs a soft-straight line to create balance and harmony for her. She will fare best in the soft-straight lines of the designers listed in that category. Elizabeth Taylor will be her most ravishing in clothing from designers who favor a curved line in their collections.

Nancy Reagan's wardrobe has been in the news time and time again. Everyone interested in fashion knows by now that Adolfo is one of her favorite designers. Interestingly, whether she is aware of it or not, she understands her body line very well. Adolfo designs tend to have very straight lines and details, and a minimum of texture.

In January of '85, Mrs. Reagan appeared on the cover of *Time* magazine in a red dress with soft lines. Two weeks later she was again photographed in a red dress, this time in the straight-lined dress with standup collar that she wore for her husband's inaugural speech. The difference in her appearance was stunning. As one observer pointed out in a later "letter to the editor," the first dress "looked like it came from K-Mart." She may have chosen the dress to make her look more approachable—more like "middle America," but how sad! That's hardly the look we hope for, whether we shop at K-Mart or Saks Fifth Avenue. Remember, once you find your right line you will be on your way to looking successful, credible, and fabulous. *It isn't how much you spend on your clothing, but how knowledgeable you are in selecting what is right for you.*

When I completed my study of body and clothing lines, I was finally able to understand why that Chanel jacket, pinstriped suit, and shirtwaist dress looked wrong on me. Each of these pieces has a very straight line. In order to complement my body and facial features, I needed a soft-straight line in my clothing. The straight-lined clothing looked stiff and rigid instead of like a natural extension of me. But—and this is an important "but"—I did not have to give up my suit, my tailored jacket, or my classic shirtwaist dress. I now shop for a jacket with a slightly curved edge, a shirtwaist dress with a shawl collar, and a suit in a soft tweed instead of a pin stripe.

Now that you know the direction of your line (straight or curved) to use in selecting your clothing, the width of your line (fine to broad), the depth of your line (the amount of texture), and the print design, let's look at the Clothing Lines chart, which summarizes this information. Also included for your reference is a Fabric Types chart.

Fabric Types Chart

- *Bouclé*—A slightly nubby wool or wool blend knit fabric. The surface finish has small loops or curls.

- *Broadcloth*—A tightly woven smooth fabric, usually of cotton or cotton blends.

- *Challis*—soft, light-to-medium-weight fabric with a diagonal twill-like weave. It is made in wool, cotton, rayon, or a blend.

- *Chiffon*—a sheer, lightweight, flowing fabric, usually in silk or silk blend, which drapes well.

- *Crepe*—a lightweight fabric of silk, wool, or blend with a slightly raised or finely puckered surface. The surface creates a matte finish.

- *Crepe de Chine*—a soft, lightweight crepe of silk or silk-blend fabric with a slightly raised surface. The surface has a matte finish.

- *Flannel*—a cotton or wool fabric that is medium to heavy in weight with a slightly fuzzy and matte surface. The fuzzy and soft surface makes the fabric moderately soft.

- *Gabardine*—a tightly woven diagonal twill weave that comes in all weights. It is generally a wool or wool blend but may be found in cotton. Because of the tight weave it is stiffer than a flannel.

- *Jersey*—a soft fine knit of cotton, wool, or blend that has a matte finish and falls softly.

- *Linen*—a fabric with a defined weave because of the sturdy threads. It comes in all weights. It tends to be stiff unless used on the bias or in flared styles; the lightest weight is called handkerchief linen.

Clothing Lines Chart

Line width	Straight	Soft-Straight	Curved
Fine	lightweight fabrics that are stiff	lightweight fabrics that fall softly	lightweight, flat, fine fabric
	top-stitching at edge	loosely woven	fine, small buttons and details
	tightly woven fabric	small, buttons, details, and trim	fabrics that drape
	small buttons, details, and trim	top-stitching at edge	top-stitching at edge
Average	average-weight fabrics, stiff, crisp, and tightly woven	average-weight fabric woven to fall in soft straight lines	average-weight fabrics that drape easily
	average-size detail and trims	average-size buttons and trim	average-size buttons and detail
	well defined top-stitching	top-stitching; not at edge, subtly defined	no top-stitching
			top-stitching on edge
Broad	medium-to-heavy-weight fabrics, stiff and tightly woven	heavy, loosely woven fabric	medium-weight fabric
	large buttons, trims, and detail	large buttons, trim, and detail	large details and trim
	double or large top-stitching	double top-stitching	no top-stitching
Texture	little to none	maximum amount	little or none

Chart continues on next page

Clothing Lines Chart (*continued.*)

Line width	Straight	Soft-Straight	Curved
Fabric Type	gabardine	linen	crepe
	linen	Thai silk	challis
	twill	challis	raw silk
	silk	tweed	jersey
	Thai silk	satin	chiffon
	taffeta	jersey	satin
	satin	wool flannel	
	moire	raw silk	
	polished cotton		
	pique		
Prints	geometric	paisley	floral
	abstract	plaid	watercolor
	modern	animal motif	realistic
	sharp plaid	realistic	rounded
	check	natural scene	swirl
	houndstooth	check	scroll
	herringbone	tweed	

Scale

PART IV

SCALE

Let's Talk About Scale (and Proper Fit)

Now that you have selected the best line for your clothing, including the right print and correct amount of texture, it's time to consider the next characteristic of style, which is scale. Scale can make the difference between looking elegant, sophisticated, and fashionable, and looking ordinary. Even though you may not be ready for high fashion, you should strive for a fashionable and current look.

Scale is not something that we have consciously been made aware of. We have all heard people say, "I can wear a smaller size if the garment is expensive," or "in designer clothes, I can buy a size smaller." The difference, however, is less size than scale. Let's take a look at what I mean by scale, overscale, and proper fit.

Webster defines scale as "a certain relative or proportionate size" or "the proportion that the representation of one object bears to another." The second definition, "the proportion that one objects bears to another" is what

I am talking about with respect to style. The first object is you; the second is your clothing. The scale of one should be in proportion to the other.

What proportion is best? The *balanced* proportion—when your clothing looks not only as though it fits you perfectly, but also looks expensive and elegant. This right proportion also has the ability to help you look thinner if you are a little overweight and to add some weight if you are too thin.

Wherever I travel in the world, I notice that European women tend to look well-dressed and elegant. Their clothing invariably looks beautiful—superbly tailored and well-balanced. They seem to understand proportion, and have traditionally preferred quality to quantity. They look for quality in fabric, construction, design, and fit. One quality silk blouse, they would insist, is a hundred times better than five inexpensive imitations. These women understand that clothes must be what I call expensively or elegantly loose.

American women are the biggest offenders when it comes to preferring quantity over quality. For some reason we have the misconception that we need an extensive wardrobe to look well-dressed. How can we possibly wear the same blouse to the office twice in one week? This way of thinking about fashion, however, is nonsense! It is far better to wear the same beautiful blouse every other day as long as it makes you look and feel great than to wear a different one each day of the week in which you feel and look ordinary.

There are several things to look for in a well-made, quality piece of clothing. Here is a chart with points to check when selecting clothing:

Quality Construction

- **Seams**
  inside seam allowance should be at least ⅝"
  seams should be finished with zig-zag or clean finished
  seam line should not pull or wrinkle but should "hang straight"
  no thread should be loose
  exterior stitching should be even, straight with no loose threads

- **Interfacing and facings**
  should not wrinkle, gap, or pull
  should be sewn in rather than fused
  inside facings should have top-stitching or be on bias

- **Hemlines**
  must hang evenly and straight
  must be finished with tape or clean finished on edge
  stitching must be loose and should not pull
  stitching should not be visible

- **Pockets**
  must be straight
  must be clean finished
  must lie flat

- **Buttons and buttonholes**
  buttons should be bone, leather, or covered (replace plastic buttons)
  buttonholes should not have loose threads
  tailor-made buttonholes must be straight

- **Belts**
  replace self-fabric belts with leather or woven belts
  do not use plastic belts; one neutral leather belt is better than any plastic

- **Thread**
  color must match exactly
  should not be clear plastic
  thread should be same type as fabric

Chart continues on next page.

- **Jackets**
  should be fully or half-lined if wool
  bottom hem should be straight
  collar should lie flat
  collar and lapel edges should lie flat, not buckle or curl
  top-stitching must be even

- **Fabrics**
  prints and plaids must be matched at all seams
  fabrics should be natural or blends that look like natural
    fabric

Small is (not necessarily) beautiful

American women also seem to have a horrible obsession with wearing clothes that don't fit and buying the smallest size possible. If we can squeeze into a size six instead of our usual size eight, we must be getting thinner! Psychologically we feel good—or do we? Small looks cheap and skimpy and makes you look heavier because you can see the bulges. Or it makes you seem too thin because your bones show.

I have a friend whose attitude illustrates this passion for small sizes perfectly. She considers any garment above a size eight unacceptable. Whenever I buy a dress or jacket and share the joy of my newfound treasure with her, her response is never, "it looks wonderful on you," or "the color is beautiful," or even "how much did it cost?" Her consuming interest is always "what size is it??" Don't envy the woman who prides herself on wearing a size two; instead, emulate the woman who wears the proper size clothing for her body regardless of its numerical designation.

Learn to recognize the dividing line between elegant and too-tight or cheap. Notice that proper fit is neither overly roomy nor snug. It is simply the right proportion. Instead of being concerned about what size clothing you buy, focus on how it fits. This chart can help you determine your proper fit:

Proper Fit: for standard pieces of clothing

- **Blouse**

set-in sleeve: when you reach for shoulder bone or top of shoulder, seam should be at, or just outside of shoulder bone (not inside)

sleeve length should be at wrist bone

sleeve width: there should be at least 1½" of double fabric when you reach up and pinch the sleeve away from your upper arm

buttons must remain closed with at least 1" of fabric on each side of bustline

at midriff there should be 2" of double fabric as you reach up and pinch the fabric from each side (this will allow for proper blousing)

length of blouse should be no shorter than hipbone

- **Skirt**

pleats should never pull open; there should be no crease or pull across break of leg

pockets must remain closed and should not pull open

straight skirts should hang from buttocks in a straight line and not curve under

skirt should not ride up when you sit

hip line: there should be at least 1" of extra fabric when you pull the skirt from your body at hip line

waistband should be loose enough to allow for two fingers to be inserted

thighs must not show; you should be able to easily turn your skirt around your body

panty line must not show

Chart continues on the next page.

• Jacket

shoulder should be at least 1″ wider than shoulder bone

collar must not wrinkle across back

when buttoned, the coat should allow for sweater or blouse
    and still not pull across shoulder or hip. There should be
    1½″ of extra fabric at midriff

sleeve length should allow for ½″ to ¼″ of blouse sleeve to
    show

sleeve width should allow for blouse or sweater, and still have
    ½″ of extra fabric

back: there should be no pull across back

pockets must remain closed; any pleat or dart must lie flat

• Slacks

pleats must remain closed

zippers and closings must lie flat

pants leg should fall straight from hip with no curve under
    at buttocks

pockets should not gap or pull open

hip: there must be at least 1 to 1½″ of fabric when you pull
    the fabric from your hip bone

waist should be big enough to allow the fingers to be in-
    serted

panty line must not show

NOTE: Jacket, skirt, and slack lengths will be covered later.

Scale

What Does "Overscale" Mean?

Now that we have defined scale in terms of fit, let's consider the term "overscale." Some of our most famous designers create clothing that is big, loose, and roomy. This is how I define overscale, which must be considered for balance and proportion as well as for a distinctive fashion look. Who can wear overscale clothing?

Let's first consider the overscale look itself apart from the look as a fashion trend. Most of the designers who create overscale clothing design for people who are tall and thin. Since we are looking for a balance with body size, we'll visualize the person who is 5'8" tall and very thin.

She probably has very long arms and legs and looks willowy—even, at times, lanky. If you saw her in her bikini you might think of her as "all arms and legs" and a bit out of proportion. So you see, all of you people out there who are short or average in height, the tall, thin model is not so perfect after all. I have just labeled her "out of proportion." In order to make her seem *in* proportion, she needs clothes that are out of proportion—

overscale—by normal standards. The resulting picture is one of balance and harmony. (If she wears a normally scaled outfit, a Chanel jacket or standard blazer, it will look skimpy and she will appear to overpower her clothing. She may seem too thin or too tall.) Tall women like Jane Fonda, Princess Diana, and Nancy Kissinger need the elegantly loose-fitting overscale look. They need the fuller cut to balance their height, and their long arms and legs. This overscaling must be in the body and torso of the garment as well as in the lengths of sleeves, jackets, skirts, and slacks.

I too am 5'8" tall, and am making progress in finding my best look. I know that I look awkward and out of proportion in clothing that is not overscale, and that I need longer jackets and skirts, fuller blouses, and wider shoulders to balance my long arms and legs.

It is very difficult for the woman who is under 5'6" tall to wear clothing by designers who design for tall models. She actually looks much better in clothing that is proportioned for her scale —in skirt lengths, sleeve lengths, and body proportions that are made for her height. But even though she will look lost in an overscale article of clothing, this woman is lucky. Almost all of the moderate-priced designers and manufacturers use an average scale, and even a few of the international designers do. The woman of average height thus has many more choices. She can create expensive designer looks for far less money. Jane Pauley, Pat Nixon, and Ali MacGraw are women who wear average-scale clothing.

The woman who is short is likely to have more difficulty finding properly scaled clothing than her tall counterpart. Occasionally, however, designers and manufacturers produce clothing in size two, which is in effect scaled down. Many are now designing a special petite scale with shorter arms, skirt lengths, shoulders, and midriffs. The total body is scaled down, which is important for a balanced look.

Styles oriented to the Orient

In Japan, where 95 percent of the population is short by American and European standards, many of the women wear clothing by designers of overscale clothing. Most of them look wonderful and there is a reason for this. Designers rarely export directly to Japan. They license their designs to Japanese manufacturers who then make clothing to Japanese scale. When I first tried to buy clothes in Japan, even those by U.S. designers such as Calvin Klein, Geoffrey Beene, and Liz Claiborne were too small for me. They were scaled down for a shorter, smaller person. Perhaps we will see more designers using differing scales so that we will all have an opportunity to have a wider choice and selection in the future.

Just as leading designers favor a particular line, they also favor a particular scale. Your height will be the major deciding factor in determining the scale of your clothing. If you are 5'3" or shorter, you will have to look for a small or petite scale. If you are 5'3" to 5'6" you will need an average scale, and if you are 5'7" or taller, you will need to look for overscale designs. The individual who has exceptionally long arms and legs for her height may occasionally be able to wear a scale larger than her height would suggest.

This list groups various-priced designers and manufacturers by the scale they tend to use.

- **Overscale**

  Giorgio Armani
  Perry Ellis
  Calvin Klein
  Anne Klein II
  Tahari
  Alexander Julian
  Donna Karan

  Gianni Versace
  Perry Ellis Portfolio
  Calvin Klein Classifications
  Norma Kamali
  Willi Wear
  Pierre Cardin
  Complice
  Claude Montana
  Carol Horn

- **Average Scale**

  Chanel
  St. John
  Castleberry
  Christian Dior
  Liz Claiborne
  Yves St. Laurent
  Albert Nipon

  Adolfo
  Jaeger
  Jones of New York
  Pendleton
  Prophecy
  Mary McFadden
  Ellen Tracy
  Carol Little

- **Petite**

  Evan Picone
  Liz Claiborne
  Joannie Char
  Country Sophisticates (Pendleton)

  Albert Nipon
  Flora Kung
  Maggie London

Notice the same garment in three different scales:

| *Petite* | *Average* | *Overscale* |

Balancing the scale

It is important to note that scale is also a vital factor in the print and design of the fabric. Those who need an overscale piece of clothing look better in prints that are large to medium in size. A small Laura Ashley print on a big overscale blouse is out of balance. For the average-scale garment, a medium to small-sized print works well. The small scale or petite size is more balanced with a small design.

I am sure you are all familiar with the petite and vivacious lady who specializes in wearing dresses with botantical prints so large that a single stamen and petal must be continued on the back. Although she adores her large swirled prints, she would look more balanced and far more elegant in smaller proportioned prints, especially if they were also complementary to her body line. She would never make this often costly mistake if she selected her correct line and scale in her print as well as in the construction of her clothing.

The Importance of the Right Accessories

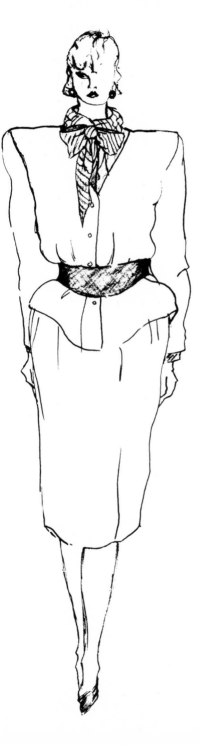

A friend of mine who has owned and managed several retail stores once told me that the first things she notices about a new customer are her shoes and handbag. She admits that the degree of salesmanship she uses with a customer is strongly influenced by not only the quality of her accessories, but their appropriateness. I'm sure she understands, without definition, the rules of my continuum line and scale proportions. How unbalanced Nancy Kissinger would look carrying a small round clutch bag. How overwhelmed Elizabeth Taylor would be by an enormous square tote.

With accessories, one has a golden opportunity to completely personalize and individualize an outfit. Have you ever been horrified by having someone show up at a particular event wearing the same dress or suit you had on? Perhaps hers looked different or even better than yours. (Some people have a real knack of adding a fabulous or even an unexpected accessory that makes the outfit stand out in the crowd.) Her secret, of course, is that she maintains the same line and scale in her accessories as she does in her clothing. She emphasizes her angles, or complements her curves. That single fabulous belt buckle, earring, or necklace in her line will often make the difference between ordinary and spectacular.

Those who need straight or sharp-straight lines in their clothing should also look for straight lines in all of their accessories. Handbags should be square or rectangular in shape and have a stiff construction. An envelope or briefcase looks fabulous when used with straight lines. A soft rounded pouch would not be consistent with straight lines of clothing and therefore would detract from the impact of an otherwise striking outfit. With soft-straight lines, either an unconstructed soft pouch or an envelope of soft leather would create a balanced look. The curved line needs a soft leather bag with small gathers, or a bag with a round or curved bottom, sides, or details.

Don't underestimate the importance of something as seemingly insignificant as a belt buckle. Square, rectangular, and geometric belt buckles are best used with straight lines. A smooth curve, oval, and shell complement a soft straight line. Circles, flowers, and swirls enhance a curved line.

Since large-size earrings are now more credible in the corporate world as well as more chic in the fashion world, it is essential that they be consistent with the lines of your face. Square, rectangular, and triangular are wonderful with faces with straight lines, while rounded and curved earrings are best on faces with curves.

Notice the examples of the types of accessories for each line type.

Straight lines:

Soft-Straight lines:

Curved lines:

Varying the classic look

Everyone can wear classic pieces of jewelry such as pearls and chains. Those who need sharp-straight lines may find that baroque pearls work better than round or that a clasp that has a geometric shape will complement their facial shape better. Pearls in combination with chains or other beads also look less curved. Often a pearl earring can be set in a gold or silver geometric setting to create the right balance of size as well as line. There are many types of chains available. Some have heavy geometric links; others are finer and the links are more curved. It is always possible to combine different pieces of your jewelry to achieve the correct overall style.

Now that you've been shown how to work with your body size and shape and not against it, you will find it truly exciting to express your individuality—to enjoy being you while you are assured of looking fabulous. To help complete your perfect total look, let me end this section on line and scale with some final hints on how to cope with some of your minor flaws. Check these charts for suggestions and hints on how to enhance your individuality.

Helpful Hints For a Balanced Body

	Straight Lines	*Soft-Straight Lines*	*Curved Lines*
Broad shoulders (Note: shoulders should be 1½″ to 2″ wider than hips to allow for clothing to hang nicely)	an asset, emphasizing the angle	an asset; may want to soften slightly with V neck, raglan, or dolman sleeves. A softly curved shoulder pad will soften any edges.	if shoulders are square you can soften with raglan or dolman sleeve use curved scoop neckline where possible
Narrow shoulders	if your facial features are extremely angular, and body thin, your shoulders can be extended with large square pads, cap sleeves, or epaulettes	add shoulder pads, boat necks, horizontal detail at shoulders	add gathers in sleeves shoulder pads that are softly rounded soft draped boat necks
Large hips	straight dresses with no belt; chemise-style overblouse with straight bottom eased skirt as long as it falls straight on bottom to maintain straight line loosely fitted, dropped belt or dropped waist stitched-down pleats straight skirts and slacks that have pleats at waist and fall straight from hip use tightly woven fabric to maintain straight lines center seam or inverted pleat	eased, unpressed, gathered or gored skirt loose overblouse belts worn low easement or pleats in waist of slacks and skirts dresses that fall softly from shoulders	eased skirt flared skirt, soft pleats and gathers loose flowing top loose overblouse with slightly fitted waist

Scale

88

Helpful Hints For a Balanced Body (*continued.*)

	Straight Lines	*Soft-Straight Lines*	*Curved Lines*
Large bust	V necklines	V necklines	scoop necklines
	open collars—straight lapels	scoop necklines	open neck with shawl collar or curved lapels
	long sleeves (do not stop sleeve at bustline)	open collar; straight or curved lapels	fuller bust is complementary to this line—enjoy it
	no breast pockets or details at bust level	no breast pockets or vertical detail	
	vertical lines	sleeve should not stop at bustline	
Small bust	adds to the impact of the straight line	works fine with this line	bows, drapes, cowl necks and gathers will add curved fullness
	horizontal lines can be added	texture, tweed, layering will add volume	embroidery and soft details at bustline
	pockets and details at bustline	loose unconstructed tops so appropriate for this line are perfect	yokes are especially good for this line
	vertical detail at bustline	pockets and details at bustline	
Long neck	positive for this look	turtlenecks	scarves
	can add high or standup collar	high collars	necklines with bows and gathers, ruffles
	big jewelry	scarves	jewelry with curved lines
	high necklines	large jewelry	soft rolled high collars
	turtlenecks		
Short necks	open necklines	open necklines	U-shaped necks
	long necklaces	scarves tied low	open collars with bows tied low
	V necks	V or U shaped neck	

NOTE: Never try to *change* your body line, *emphasize* it!

Helpful Hints for Your Face Shape and Hairstyle

- **Diamond-shaped face**
  wonderful cheekbones that should be emphasized with angular hair styles
  may wish to add width across forehead with fullness or bangs

- **Square face**
  emphasize the angles by asymmetric styles, geometric cuts
  may wish to add height to create a balance with total body height by adding fullness on top to lengthen face

- **Rectangular face**
  emphasize angles—try asymmetric style, geometric cuts
  may wish to shorten effect with bangs and hairstyles with no fullness on top to balance body and neck lengths—an off-center part will help

- **Round face**
  emphasize curves with soft hairstyle
  may wish to add height to balance neck and body proportions—add fullness on top

- **Oblong face**
  emphasize the soft, smooth, straight lines
  may wish to use bangs and hairstyles with no height to shorten effect—an off-center part will help

- **Pear-shaped face**
  emphasize soft curves
  may wish to add fullness across forehead with soft curls to balance narrow forehead with fuller cheeks

- **Heart-shaped face**
  emphasize curves
  may use an off-center part to soften forehead and add fullness at chin level

- *Note:* Do not try to change the line of your face; learn to
  enhance it!

Your individual style now has a foundation. Now that you have some guidelines and parameters to work with to enhance your physical characteristics, let's look at ways to incorporate your personality into your individual style.

The Three Faces of Fashion ...and Overscale as a Fashion Term

What is "high" fashion? As elusive as the definition might be, there seem to be three distinct levels of fashion in the world today. High fashion can be defined as the styles that are introduced each year in Paris, Milan, and New York by the world's leading fashion designers. These designers cater to those fortunate women who have the desire and affluence to own beautifully made status clothing. The colors, fabrics, prints, and silhouettes favored by these designers are immediately copied and reinterpreted for millions of women of more limited means, who are just as interested in following current fashion trends.

The second level of fashion has more to do with the real world, where manufacturers create clothing for the great number of women who dress for their day-to-day jobs and lifestyles. These women want to look appropriately dressed and efficient as they pursue their various careers. Their clothing styles may lean toward the classic, but they keep their fashion appeal.

There is yet another group of women: the innovators. To these women, fashion means experimenting with the new and often outrageous offerings that spark the volatile fashion scene from season to season. The innovators have the personality and drive that it takes to be first with something new and different. *Which type are you?*

I contend that high fashion is really nothing more than an exaggeration of scale, line, or detail. The recent trend toward overscale clothing is an exaggeration of scale. (Some of the exaggerated looks, such as the Comme des Garçon which came from Japan several years ago, were so exaggerated that they created a sloppy and unkempt effect. Fortunately, these looks are being replaced by a more attractive exaggerated proportion.)

How much exaggeration is appropriate? In order to avoid an extreme or trendy image and still achieve an exaggerated fashion look, it is important to exaggerate the scale by one size beyond your elegantly loose fit. This year shoulders are wider, skirt lengths are very long or very short, jackets are either long or short and worn with contrasting lengths in skirts, pants are back and are tapered, baggy, or cropped. It is important to watch the trends from season to season as designers enjoy the challenge of change.*

Who can wear the exaggerated or high-fashion looks? It all depends on who you are inside. If you have the desire, personality, and knowledge to wear the look—and wear it with confidence—you can do it. You now have the knowledge to find your right line and scale. Let's find out if you have the personality to exaggerate it!

*At the end of the book I will tell you how to send for your *Always in Style Portfolio*. Each season you will receive a new edition to enable you to keep abreast of the trends. The portfolio will interpret these trends for your particular body line, so that there will be no more guessing about which of the new styles will be the most complementary for you.

A question of personality

Here are some simple questions relating to your personality. Please answer them honestly.

- Are you outgoing and extroverted?
  ☐Yes ☐No

- Are you the first in your town or group
  to try a new hairstyle?
  ☐Yes ☐No

- Do you love the unexpected?
  ☐Yes ☐No

- Do you enjoy being noticed?
  ☐Yes ☐No

- Are you sophisticated?
  ☐Yes ☐No

- Do you love clothes?
  ☐Yes ☐No

- Are you conservative and cautious?
  ☐Yes ☐No

- Have you had the same or similar hairstyle
  for several years?
  ☐Yes ☐No

- Are you satisfied with your current wardrobe?
  ☐Yes ☐No

- Are you applying your makeup the same way
  you did five years ago?
  ☐Yes ☐No

- Do you keep your skirt length
  the same year after year?
  ☐Yes ☐No

- Are you shy or reserved?
  ☐Yes ☐No

If you answered yes to the first six questions, you're ready for a high fashion look. If you answered yes to the last six, you are more conservative but still want to strive for a fashionable look. If your answers were mixed, you probably don't want to start with an extreme, but to lean in a high-fashion direction.

Remember that conservative and high fashion are not two separate looks. Instead, there is a whole spectrum from the most extreme to the most conservative, with many steps along the way. You can therefore always experiment by reaching out in a fashion direction slowly. Lengthen or shorten a skirt a little more than average, add a looser top and new belt, wear a flat shoe or a loose trouser. If it works for you and you feel comfortable, keep going. Some of you will reach further than others.

Those of you who have no desire for a high-fashion look may be comfortable with an elegantly loose fit and your proper line. That is fine, as long as you reach in the direction of the current fashion trends. You can look current and fashionable even though you are conservative. Lengthen or shorten your skirt just a little, add a new jacket, add small shoulder pads to your dress or jacket. Update your look. Those of you who want the high-fashion look will have to exaggerate more. Add a larger shoulder pad, wear skirts to your ankle or above your knee. But be sure to start with your proper fit and scale it up slowly, until you reach a maximum of one size larger than your elegantly loose fit.

As always, there are certain guidelines to consider in determining just how long or short you can wear your jackets and skirts for either a fashionably conservative or a high-fashion look and still adapt the lengths to you personally. I have already suggested scaling up your clothing by one size; now let's look at your possible lengths.

Keeping it all in proportion

We have discussed "ideal" body and facial shapes. There are also "ideal" body proportions. The ideal body is supposed to be in four equal portions, from the top of the head to the underarm; from the underarm to the break of the leg; from the break of the leg to the knee; and from the knee to the floor, as shown in this illustration.

The ideal body can be divided into four equal portions:

¼

- Top of the head to the underarm,

¼

- Underarm to the break of the leg,

¼

- Break of the leg to the knee, and

¼

- Knee to the floor.

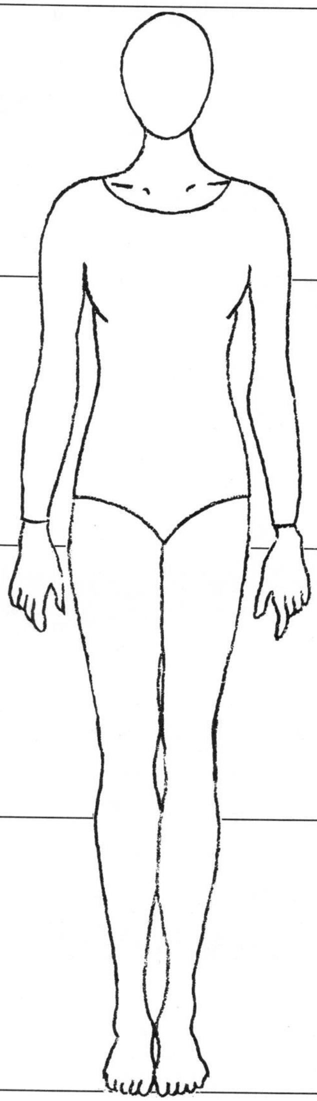

You may not be equally proportioned. By understanding where you are long or short, you will learn how to best adapt any fashion to your specific needs.

For instance, you can change how long your legs look by changing your jacket length—but how much you can change it depends on your individual proportion.

Once again, if your body is not "equally" proportioned, don't worry about trying to make it seem so. You should merely understand where you are long or short so that you know how long or short you can wear your skirts and jackets as fashion trends change.

How not to look older

The first thing to do is to decide what look you are trying to achieve. We should all look fashionable and lean in the direction of the most current looks. Many people say that they want to find one length for their skirts and jackets and keep them there forever! It is, of course, more convenient, but you will also look *outdated*. Your clothes will look like the ones you wore years ago, which will make you look older. It's like putting on your makeup the same way that you did when you first started wearing it. I often tell my classes that I can tell how old you are by the way you put on your makeup: 1950's style, 1960's, or 1940's! There's no question that it's a bit inconvenient to hem your skirts periodically, but you will look so much better, so much more youthful, and like you care about yourself. The extra time and effort are well worth it. It doesn't take much to update your clothing; it is often no more than a matter of an inch in one direction or the other.

Legs: knowing where you stand

In my line and proportion class, I sketch your body and determine which quarter of your body is long and which is short. If you are long or short from your head to your underarm, it is not critical. I am more interested in your leg length, especially from your knee down, and your torso length. Look at areas A and B on this illustration.

How can these figures wear longer skirts and still flatter their legs?

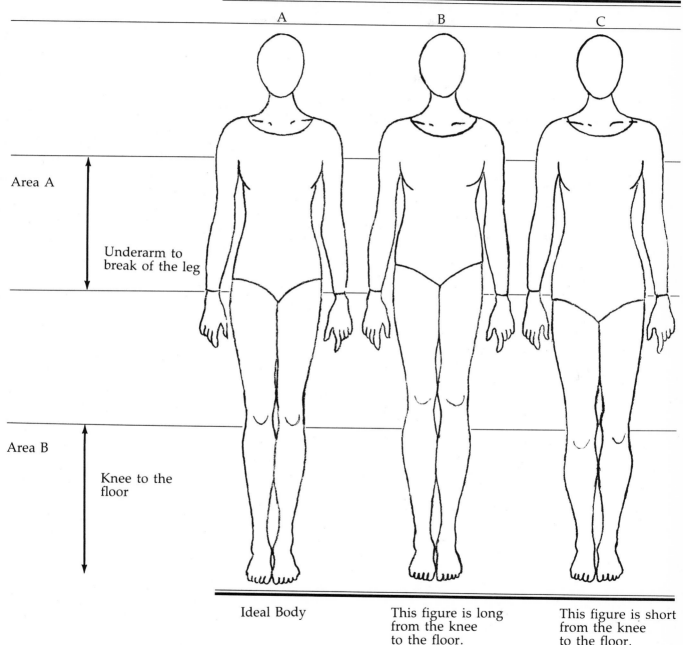

A

B

C

Area A

Underarm to break of the leg

Area B

Knee to the floor

Ideal Body

This figure is long from the knee to the floor.

This figure is short from the knee to the floor.

Let's look at the length from your knee to the floor. If your leg is long from the knee to the floor, you can wear your skirts very long when the styles are long and still have enough leg showing for the skirt to be flattering to your leg. If short skirts are in style, you must be careful. If you wear your skirt too short, your leg will look so long that it will seem out of proportion. You can achieve the look of a shorter skirt by wearing your skirt a little longer and lengthening your jacket. The result: your skirt will appear shorter. You have managed to achieve a fashionable look and still complement your leg.

If your leg is short from the knee down and you want to wear long skirts, you must be careful. In order to have enough of your leg showing for the skirt to be flattering to your leg, you can't make your skirt too long. You don't have enough room. However, you can shorten your jacket, which will make the skirt appear longer. You will be able to wear very short skirts when they are in style but you must be careful that your jacket does not get too long. We still want to see some skirt! It's all basically an optical illusion. By understanding where you are long and short, and understanding the fashion trends, you will know how to adjust your clothing lengths.

In the Chanel days the fashionable look was one of equal proportions. This too can be achieved by changing your skirt and jacket lengths. Use this information to create the look you want, rather than as a means of "judging" the perfection of your body. Your body and facial size and shape and your proportions are "you." Work with them to develop your own style.

This chart summarizes your total style. Select your right body line and fill in the blanks where necessary for your individualized set of parameters.

Total Style

	Straight Lines	Soft-Straight lines	Curved Lines
Body shapes	triangle rectangle square	rectangle ellipse	oval circle
Face shapes	diamond rectangle square	oval square oblong rectangle/softened	oval heart pear round oblong
Clothing lines	straight exterior line straight detail lines	soft-straight exterior lines straight exterior lines with soft fabric and unconstructed lines straight details on soft fabric contoured exterior lines	curved exterior lines curved details soft-straight details

FABRIC Choose one detail size in your line

	Straight Lines	Soft- Straight lines	Curved Lines
Fine fabric/ small details	☐	☐	☐
Average weight fabric/ average details	☐	☐	☐
Heavy weight fabrics/ large detail	☐	☐	☐

Chart continues on the next page.

FABRIC (*continued*)

	Straight Lines	*Soft-Straight lines*	*Curved Lines*
Texture	little	maximum	little
Print	geometric abstract stripe sharp plaid herringbone houndstooth check	stripe paisley plaid realistic tweed	floral watercolor swirl rounded

SCALE   Choose one scale in your line

	Straight Lines	*Soft-Straight lines*	*Curved Lines*
Overscale **5′7″ and over**	☐	☐	☐
Average scale **5′6″ to 5′3″**	☐	☐	☐
Petite **5′3″ and under**	☐	☐	☐
Accessories	geometric/angular constructed square diamond rectangle	geometric/soft unconstructed constructed with soft ma- terial oval ellipse	curved soft constructed round floral oval

Chart continues on the next page.

ACCESSORIES   Choose one scale of accessories for your line

	Straight Lines	Soft-Straight lines	Curved Lines
Large accessories (overscale)	☐	☐	☐
Medium (average)	☐	☐	☐
Small/medium (petite)	☐	☐	☐

FASHION DIRECTION   Choose one style direction for your line

	Straight Lines	Soft-Straight lines	Curved Lines
High fashion (exaggerated scale and accessories)	☐	☐	☐
Conservative high fashion (slight exaggeration)	☐	☐	☐
Conservative fashionable (classic with fashion direction)	☐	☐	☐

Making your choice the right choice

Today's fashion designers and manufacturers offer exciting options to each of us, whatever our body type and personal style. It is no longer a matter of designers ''dictating'' what we should wear. You and I can choose the fashion styles that best suit our own particular body type, personality, and lifestyle. Each new season brings changes that make shopping more exciting than ever, especially when you know how to incorporate them into your own personal style of dressing.

Now let's look at the final element in your total style: *Color*.

Q. *Every season the designers give us new looks and introduce new colors. How can we follow their lead and change our wardrobes each season without spending a fortune?*

A. Fashion designers give us a *direction*. Although it's important to lean in this fashion direction to look current and fashionable, no one needs to radically change her wardrobe from season to season. You only need to take a few of the many steps that lead to the latest high-fashion look. Move slowly in the season's new direction. Even a little change will make you look youthful and up-to-date. It will also make you feel good about yourself!

Q. *I have attended a "line and design" class. I have been told the best length to wear my jackets and skirts. Does that mean I should ignore the fashion trends? I don't necessarily want a high-fashion look, but I do want to look fashionable.*

A. The ideal body can be divided vertically into four equal sections: the head to the underarm, the underarm to the break of the leg, the break of the leg to the knee, and the knee to the floor. If you want to look as though you have these ideal proportions, the lengths you were given are correct. Each year, however, different proportions are considered new and exciting. (The designers change these proportions not to be difficult but because they understand the need for change in our lives.) Because in order to grow as individuals we must constantly learn and try new things, it is important to understand how to adapt your proportions to new fashion looks. By knowing where you are long or short you can better understand how to change your jacket and skirt lengths from year to year. How much will depend on your proportions, your desires, and the fashion direction.

Body Lines in Art History

Each body type has been the ideal at some point in history, and has been immortalized by artists of the period.

The early Egyptians were clear admirers of the **sharp-straight**: strong, linear body lines, angular faces, and flared shoulders were further emphasized by exaggerated slanted eyes—patterns repeated in the hieroglyphics of the era.

The flared shoulders and angularity are typical in Egyptian hieroglyphics. (sharp-straight)

Notice the strong, angular facial features, slanted eyes, long slender nose, and straight feeling to the body in this Byzantine piece, *Madonna on a Curved Throne*. The curved throne further emphasized the angularity of the figure. (straight)

Less extreme, Whistler's *White Girl* depicts straight facial features and a rectangular body line. (straight)

In the more recent 19th century work of American expressionist John Singer Sargent, broad shoulders, long bodies, and angular facial features were central characteristics of *Madame X* and *The Wyndham Sisters*.

The **straight** body line, which appeared during the Byzantine period, was delineated in the 16th century by El Greco and in the late 19th century by the stark rectangular figures of Modigliani.

Laocoön (c. 1610)
El Greco (Domenikos Theotokopoulos) (1541-1614)
Samuel H. Kress Collection
National Gallery of Art, Washington

El Greco's work illustrates the rectangular body line with its subtle, lengthened curves. By elongating his figures, he emphasizes the straight lines. (soft-straight)

The combining of straight and curved lines into the **soft-straight** body line—a rectangular body with some softness and an oval face, or a slightly curved, elliptical body with a facial shape of some squareness—is typified by Gauguin's *Tahitian Models*, Botticelli's *The Birth of Venus*, and the Degas ballerinas.

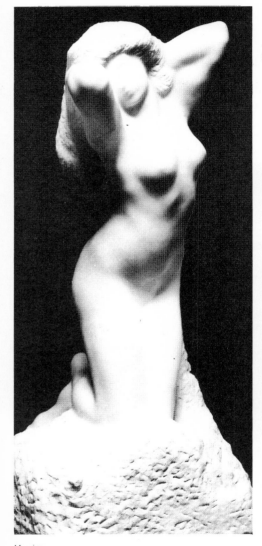

Notice the smooth contour of Rodin's marble. (soft-straight)

Gauguin shows a more rectangular body with smooth facial details. This combination projects a soft-straight line. (soft-straight)

Morning
Auguste Rodin, French (1840-1917)
marble
Gift of Mrs. John W. Simpson
National Gallery of Art, Washington

Fatata te Miti (1892)
Paul Gauguin (1830-1903)
Chester Dale Collection
National Gallery of Art, Washington

108

The **soft-curved** body line, represented by the oval, was the ideal of the ancient Greeks. Later homage to this body shape was paid by old masters Titian and Rembrandt, and French impressionist Manet.

The Degas ballerinas pictured here show neither extreme straight nor curved lines, instead conveying an over-all elliptical feeling. (soft-curved)

This figure is a clear example of the soft-curved body line.

Four Dancers
Edgar Degas (1834-1917)
Chester Dale Collection
National Gallery of Art, Washington

The Nymph of the Spring
Lucas Cranach the Elder (1472-1553)
Gift of Clarence Y. Palitz
National Gallery of Art, Washington

The full-bodied nudes of Flemish painter Peter Paul Rubens shine as examples of the **curved** body line, which is represented by the circle. Ingres and Renoir are also famed for the curves of their subjects, as was Pablo Picasso during the early days of his long career.

Curved lines are vividly portrayed in Maillol's bronze. (curved)

Here, a well-defined waist helps to emphasize the rounded curves of this Renoir nude. (curved)

Summer
Aristide Maillol, French (1861-1944)
Ailsa Mellon Bruce Fund
National Gallery of Art, Washington

Auguste Renoir, 1841-1919
Bather Arranging Her Hair, (1893)
Chester Dale Collection
National Gallery of Art, Washington

110

It is clear that there is inherent beauty in every body type. It is equally clear that fashions that incorporate the correct style, proportion, and color for you as an individual—regardless of your body type—can help you express the best of your personal beauty.

A softer curve can be seen in the round face and body of Ingres' *Madame Moitessier*. (curved)

A full, rounded, curved body and oval face show the voluptuous ideal of this period. (curved)

Venus with a Mirror
Titian (1477-1576)
Andrew W. Mellon Collection
National Gallery of Art, Washington

Madame Moitessier, 1951
Jean-Auguste-Dominique Ingres (1780-1867)
Samuel H. Kress Collection
National Gallery of Art, Washington
(No. 882/1946.7.18)

111

A Fashion Design:
The Finishing Touch

Designers must function in many areas simultaneously: they need to consider fabric, color, line, scale, and detail as well as the indefinable "something" that will give the end product the distinctive aura their clients come to expect.

Sources of design ideas are as varied as the individual designers themselves. They often come from the ingenious combinations devised by the young people of cities like London and Milan, which spawned the term "street chic." Some signature designs are repeated year after year, changing only enough to reveal the newest fashion direction. Others offer spectacular change as new talents take the industry's center stage.

Textile designers and manufactuers play a key role in the design process, interpreting the fabric direction with enticing early forecasts of color and print. As they inspire the fashion designers, these fabrics often provide the first element in the total composition.

The next step: creating the silhouette. When the new fabrics are used to interpret the new silhouette, the design begins to take form. After the final details are in place, and when the fabric, silhouette, and detail lines work together to achieve balance and harmony, the result can be stunningly successful.

Here, a designer's "blueprint" shows the parameters used in designing a collection. First two current fabric designs are selected—a paisley and a foulard—in complementary colors. Although each of the fabrics makes a statement on its own, their impact is more than doubled when they are used together.

Then the silhouette line of the garment is developed. Notice the line, scale, and detail of the drawings. Some of the silhouette lines are straight; some are curved. Separates are chosen to give the wearer a variety of options for using the individual pieces. When presented in the different fabrics, each piece changes, becoming softer in the paisley and "straighter" in the foulard. The collection then becomes suitable for a large, varied clientele.

When is the design "finished"? Let's look at this question from the designer's point of view. The ultimate factor then becomes who will actually *wear* the design. Ideally, this individual will have the physical characteristics and personality to truly complement the designer's creation. Its full beauty—*and that of the wearer*—can only be realized when one complements the other.

A Designers Blueprint

WINTER

WINTER → Summer

WINTER → Autumn

WINTER → Spring

Soft
Fuchsia
(Summer)

Teal
Blue
(Autumn)

Emerald
Turquoise
(Spring)

New Colors for Winters: Your Flow Colors

Lipstick and Blush Shades

WINTER → *Autumn*

Notice the movement from plum to russet with the deep true red in the center.

WINTER → *Summer*

Notice the movement from bright fuchsia to soft dusty pink with the raspberry in the center.

WINTER → *Spring*

Notice the movement from blue-red to coral with the watermelon in the center.

Colors for an Expanded Wardrobe

WINTER → *Summer*

The Soft Fuchsia is blue-based and deep enough for the Winter/Summer to wear successfully.

WINTER → *Autumn*

The Teal Blue has the right intensity and a blue-green tone. It therefore works well for the Winter/Autumn.

WINTER → *Spring*

The Emerald Turquoise is a bright clear color with a blue-green quality. It looks fabulous on the Winter/Spring.

WINTER → Autumn   Patricia

WINTER → Summer   Susan

WINTER → Spring   Joan

There are Many Types of Winters

WINTER → Autumn

Patricia has deep coloring. Her dark brown eyes have a hint of green in them. Her dark brown hair has red highlights. Since her skintone is blue based, the muted and most golden of the autumn colors are not her best.

WINTER → Summer

Susan has a rosy complexion. Her eyes are gray-blue and her hair is medium brown. Her cool coloring is neither very dark nor very light. This cool undertone is her most dominant characteristic. She has coloring similar to some Summers.

WINTER → Spring

Joan has porcelain skin, dark brown hair, and bright clear blue eyes. Her most dominant color characteristic is her brightness. She has coloring similar to some Springs.

New Colors for Summers: Your Flow Colors

Lipstick and Blush Shades

SUMMER → Winter

Notice the movement from dusty pink to bright fuchsia with the raspberry in the center.

SUMMER → Spring

Notice the movement from rose to clear salmon with the true and warm pinks in the center.

SUMMER → Autumn

Notice the movement from muted burgundy to soft mahogany with the dusty warm pinks in the center.

Colors for an Expanded Wardrobe

SUMMER → Winter

The Deep Hot Pink is not too bright for a Summer/Winter to wear. It is medium in intensity and very flattering.

SUMMER → Autumn

The Grayed Green has a soft, muted look with very little yellow. It has a pastel-like quality and therefore looks wonderful on the Summer/Autumn.

SUMMER → Spring

The Clear Bright Aqua does not have a predominance of yellow and looks exciting on the Summer/Spring.

Deep Hot Pink
(Winter)

Grayed Green
(Autumn)

Clear Bright Aqua
(Spring)

SUMMER → Winter — Laurie

SUMMER → Autumn — Valerie

There are Many Types of Summers

Summers are the ones who can most successfully frost their hair. All three of these Summers have frosted hair.

SUMMER → Winter

Laurie's natural hair color is a medium ash brown. She has a rosy complexion, and deep blue eyes. Her cool coloring is deeper and brighter than many Summers.

SUMMER → Autumn

Valerie also has medium ash brown hair. However, her eyes are a soft, warm green. Her complexion is not as obviously cool as Laurie's. Her dominant characteristic is her muted coloring, like some Autumns.

SUMMER → Spring

Lori's coloring is light. She has light blonde hair with some warm highlights and blue eyes. Her complexion is cool, but similiar to Springs.

SUMMER → Spring — Lori

117

New Colors for Autumns: Your Flow Colors

Lipstick and Blush Shades

AUTUMN → Spring
Notice the movement from deep russet to light coral with the bittersweet in the center.

AUTUMN → Winter
Notice the movement from russet to plum with the deep true red in the center.

AUTUMN → Summer
Notice the movement from soft mahogany to muted burgundy with the dusty warm pink in the center.

Colors for an Expanded Wardrobe

AUTUMN → Winter
True Red is a deep color that complements the Autumn/Winter person.

AUTUMN → Summer
Deep Blue-Green has enough yellow in it and is the right intensity for the Autumn/Summer person.

AUTUMN → Spring
The Light Clear Gold is very golden and soft enough to look special on the Autumn/Spring.

True Red (Winter)

Deep Blue Green (Summer)

Light Clear Gold (Spring)

AUTUMN → Winter   Jeannie

AUTUMN → Summer   Phyllis

AUTUMN → Spring   Jennifer

There are Many Types of Autumns

AUTUMN → Winter

Jeannie has ivory skin, dark warm brown eyes, and deep auburn hair. The depth of her coloring is her most dominant characteristic. She has coloring similar to some Winters.

AUTUMN → Summer

Phyllis has medium golden blonde hair and green eyes. Her coloring is neither very dark nor very light. Her most dominant characteristic is the softness of her coloring, which is similar to some Summers.

AUTUMN → Spring

Jennifer has auburn hair, moss green eyes, and a golden complexion. She radiates golden. Her most dominant characteristic is her warm undertone. She has coloring similar to some Springs.

SPRING

SPRING → *Autumn*

SPRING → *Summer*

SPRING → *Winter*

New Colors for Springs: Your Flow Colors

Lipstick and Blush Shades

SPRING → *Autumn*
Notice the movement from coral to russet with the bittersweet in the center.

SPRING → *Summer*
Notice the movement from clear salmon to rose with the true and warm pinks in the center.

SPRING → *Winter*
Notice the movement from coral to blue-red with the watermelon in the center.

Colors for an Expanded Wardrobe

SPRING → *Autumn*
The Pumpkin of Autumn is light and bright enough to complement the Spring/Autumn.

SPRING → *Summer*
The Watermelon has a slight touch of Coral and is often referred to as the "orange" of Summer. It is thus a wonderful Spring/Summer color.

SPRING → *Winter*
The Chinese Blue is bright and clear with enough yellow in it to look fabulous on the Spring/Winter.

Pumpkin
(Autumn)

Watermelon
(Summer)

Chinese Blue
(Winter)

SPRING → Winter   Carol Ann

SPRING → Autumn   Sharon

There are Many
Types of Springs

SPRING → Winter

Carol Ann has dark brown hair and bright clear blue eyes. Her ivory complexion is very bright and is in strong contrast to her dark hair. The brightness of her coloring is her most dominant characteristic. She has coloring similar to some Winters.

SPRING → Autumn

Sharon has bright red hair, turquoise eyes, and golden skin. Her most dominant characteristic is her golden coloring, which is similar to many Autumns.

SPRING → Summer

Holly's coloring is light. She has a warm pink complexion, light golden blonde hair, and warm blue eyes. Her coloring is similar to some Summers.

SPRING → Summer   Holly

121

COOL CHART

Winter/ Summer

In the cool chart of Winter/Summer, the colors are arranged from the deepest and most vivid of Winter on the left, to the softest and most muted of Summer on the right. Notice the colors in the center band.

ROW I: The soft white of Summer is the white that can be worn successfully by everyone. The medium grays of Winter and the blue-grays of Summer are in the same range. The charcoal gray of Winter becomes the black of the middle-band colors.

ROW III: The blues in the Winter flow section are the true blue and the navy. However, the navy will not be as deep as it is in the true Winter palette. The periwinkle of Summer is added in spite of the fact that it is lighter than the other band colors because it is clear enough to work well.

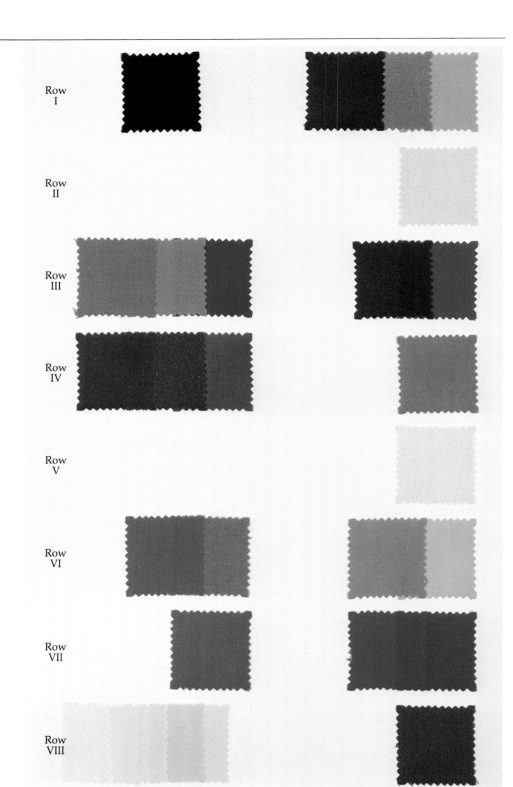

Row I

Row II

Row III

Row IV

Row V

Row VI

Row VII

Row VIII

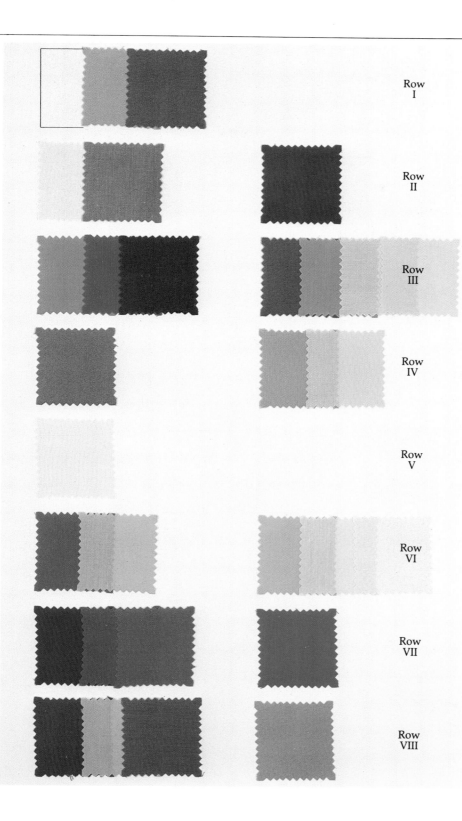

Row
I

Row
II

Row
III

Row
IV

Row
V

Row
VI

Row
VII

Row
VIII

ROW IV & V: The greens and yellows are closely related.

ROW VI: The medium pinks of Winter and the rose pink of Summer appear to be almost interchangeable. The deep rose of Summer is a little more muted than some of the other band colors but the depth and richness make it right.

ROW VII: The burgundies, blue-reds, and raspberry are truly flow colors.

ROW VIII: The plum, orchid, and fuchsia of Summer are medium to dark in intensity and the clearest of the Summer colors.

WARM CHART

Autumn/ Spring

In the warm chart of Autumn/Spring, the colors are arranged from the deepest and most muted of Autumn on the left, to the lightest and clearest of Spring on the right. Look at the colors in the center band.

ROW I: The oyster, beige, and camel of Autumn are very similar to the ivory and tans of Spring.

ROW II: The yellow-gold, terra cotta, and pumpkin of Autumn are light and clear enough not to appear too heavy next to Spring's light clear gold and golden brown.

ROW III: The salmon and peach of Autumn, although more muted than the salmon and peach of Spring, are still light enough to be in the same range.

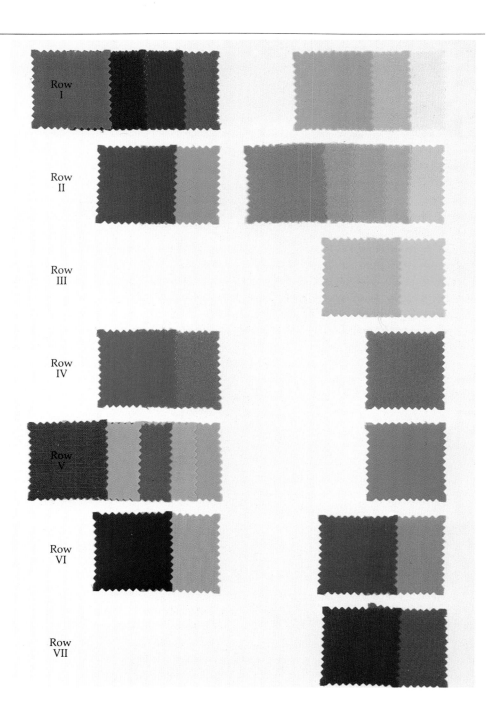

Row I

Row II

Row III

Row IV

Row V

Row VI

Row VII

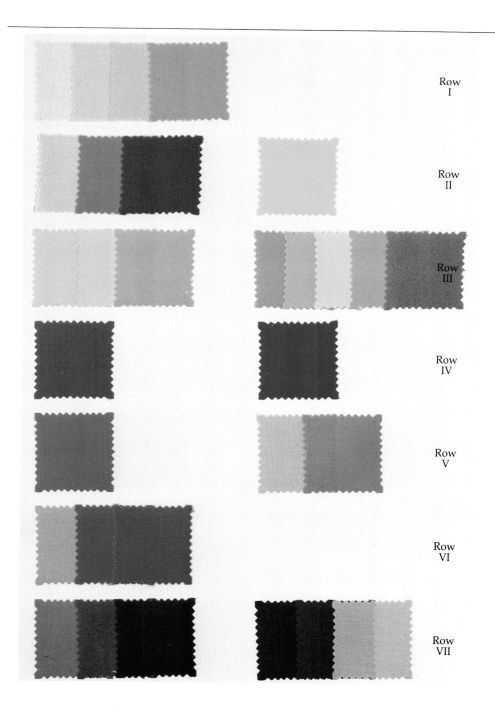

Row
I

Row
II

Row
III

Row
IV

Row
V

Row
VI

Row
VII

ROW IV: The orange-reds of Autumn and Spring are essentially interchangeable. It is possible to include the bittersweet of Autumn in this center band.

ROW V: The greens included from both palettes are bright and clear.

ROW VI: The teals, turquoises, and aquas of each season are as clearly related as the beiges.

ROW VII: The periwinkle and purple of Autumn are only slightly deeper than Spring's periwinkle and violet but are clear and light enough to be in the flow range.

DEEP CHART

Winter/ Autumn

In the deep chart of Winter/Autumn, the colors are arranged from the deepest and bluest of Winter on the left, to the most muted and golden of Autumn on the right. Look at the center-band colors.

ROW 1: Notice that the deep brown of Autumn is very dark, not particularly golden, and works well with black accessories. Black and charcoal are included in the flow band as neutrals. The mahogany is a cross between rust and burgundy and therefore fits appropriately in the band. Because some rusts are clear and contain more red than orange, that rust is included.

ROW II: To oyster and taupe, Summer's soft white can be added.

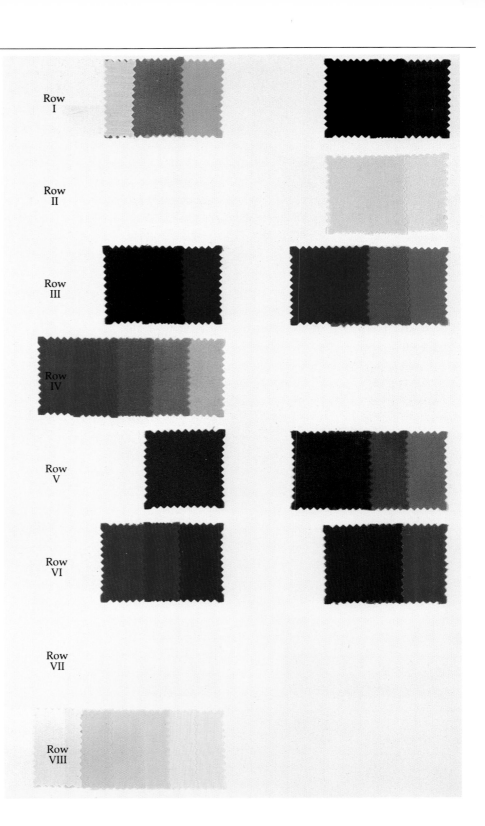

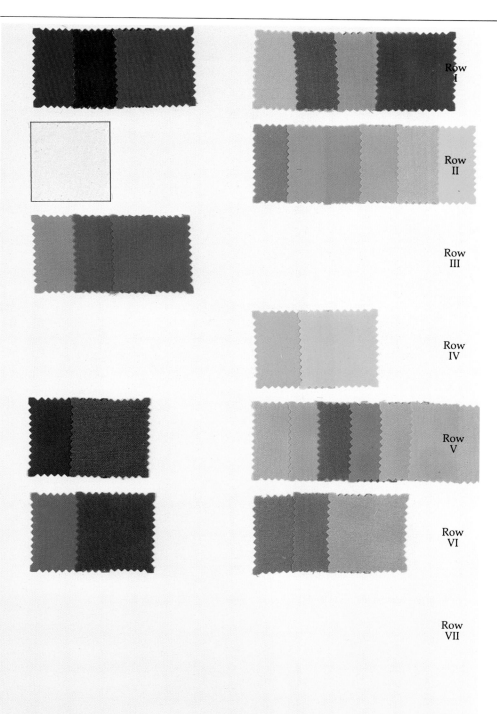

Row
I

Row
II

Row
III

Row
IV

Row
V

Row
VI

Row
VII

Row
VIII

ROW III: The turquoise and Chinese blue of Winter contain some yellow in the base and are appropriately included. The teal and turquoise of Autumn create a blue-green effect. The periwinkle is blue and clear enough to be worn with the Winter colors.

ROW V: The true greens of Winter and the pine green are obviously similar to the forest green of Autumn. The olive is the most muted but the intensity and the "gray" effect make it work.

ROW VI: The true red of Winter has equal amounts of gold and blue and therefore is directly related to the tomato red of Autumn. The purples are almost interchangeable in the intensity comparison.

LIGHT CHART

Summer/
Spring

In the light chart of Summer/Spring, the colors are arranged from the bluest of Summer on the left, to the most golden of Spring on the right. Again, observe the center band.

ROW I: The ivory and buff of Spring are yellow-based but clear. The soft white and light lemon yellow are clear and blend well with the Spring palette.

ROW II: The blue-greens of Summer contain yellow and are clear enough to work with the Spring band colors.

ROW III: The pinks of Spring are warm pinks, with a hint of yellow, and therefore look very similar to the true pinks of Summer. The deep rose is the darkest color in the band but has a slight warm tone.

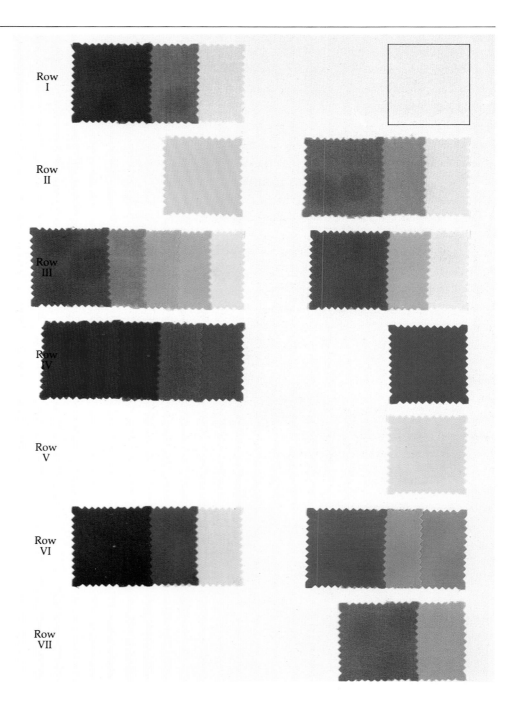

Row I

Row II

Row III

Row IV

Row V

Row VI

Row VII

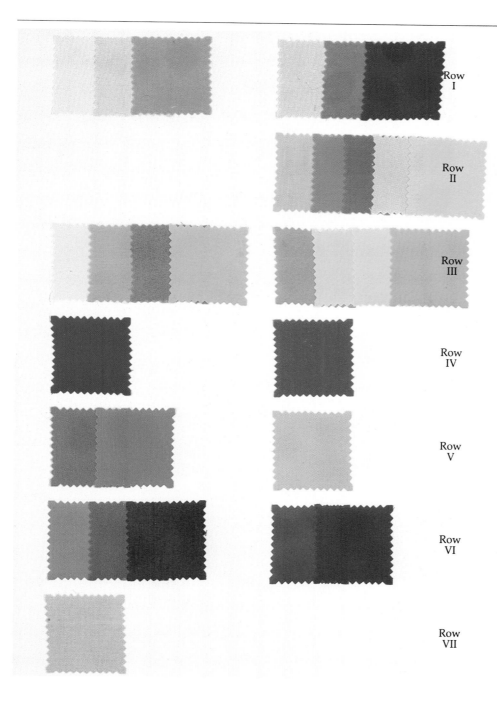

ROW IV: The light true red of Spring contains both blue and gold. The watermelon of Summer actually has a touch of coral in it, and is often referred to as Summer's orange.

ROW V: Spring's emerald turquoise is a blue-green and is therefore closely related to the blue-green of Summer. The turquoises included do not have a strong yellow base.

ROW VI: Any periwinkle is compatible with both seasons and cannot be omitted. The medium blue of Summer and the light clear navy of Spring are similar and not too dark to be included in the band.

ROW VII: The medium true gray of Winter is an excellent color to be added to the center band since it is not too deep and does not contain an excess of blue. It is a wonderful flow color for both seasons.

MUTED CHART

Summer/ Autumn

In the muted chart of Summer/Autumn, the colors are arranged from the bluest of Summer on the left, to the most golden of Autumn on the right.

ROW I: Look at the band colors and notice the browns. The Autumn browns are neither too dark nor especially golden. They are very similar to the cocoa and rose-brown of Summer. The soft white and oyster are closely related; the oyster is a little deeper. The mahogany of Autumn is a muted brown-burgundy and works with many colors in the Summer band. As it becomes more soft and muted, it becomes a better flow color.

ROW III: The greens of Autumn are soft, muted, and greyed. They have an almost pastel quality to them. The forest green is a bit dark, but as it is grayed down, it works well as a flow color. The blue-greens of Summer are the yellowest of the Summer colors and work with the many greens of Autumn.

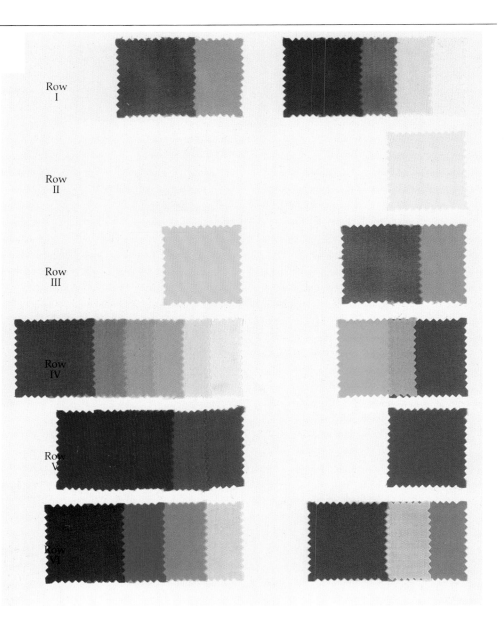

Row I

Row II

Row III

Row IV

Row V

Row VI

130

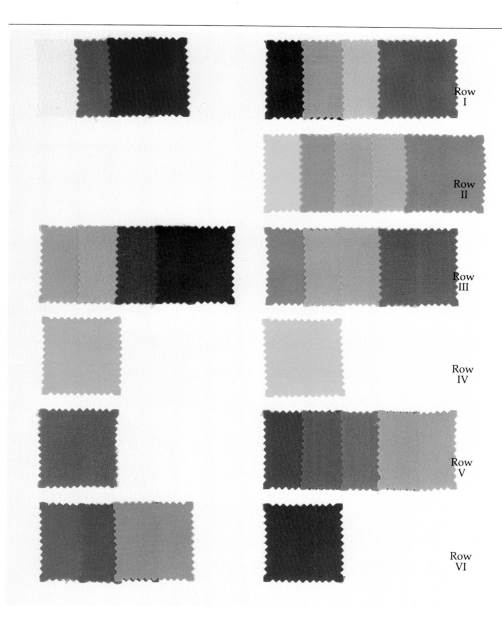

Row I

Row II

Row III

Row IV

Row V

Row VI

ROW IV: The salmon of Autumn has a warm pink tone as does the rose of Summer. The rose pink and the deep rose are soft and muted.

ROW V: The bittersweet of Autumn is muted, not too deep or golden. The watermelon of Summer has a touch of coral to it and works well, as it did in the Summer/Spring chart.

ROW VI: The periwinkles are interchangeable as in most of the charts. The teal of Autumn is muted and is blue-green in tone. The more muted it is, the better it will be as a flow color. The turquoises included are muted and not exceptionally golden. It is amazing to see not only the softness of the color in the flow chart, but the similarities in the band colors when comparing something as subtle as degree of clarity.

BRIGHT CHART

Winter/Spring

In the bright chart of Winter/Spring, the colors have been arranged from the deepest and bluest of Winter on the left, to the lightest and most golden of Spring on the right. Notice the center-band colors.

ROW I: The ivory and taupe are closely related. Since the ivory is often very golden, substituting the oyster of Autumn or the soft white of Summer are excellent options.

ROW II: The light and medium grays of Winter are true colors, which are not too dark and work beautifully as flow neutrals. The warm gray is clear enough to be included with the grays of Winter.

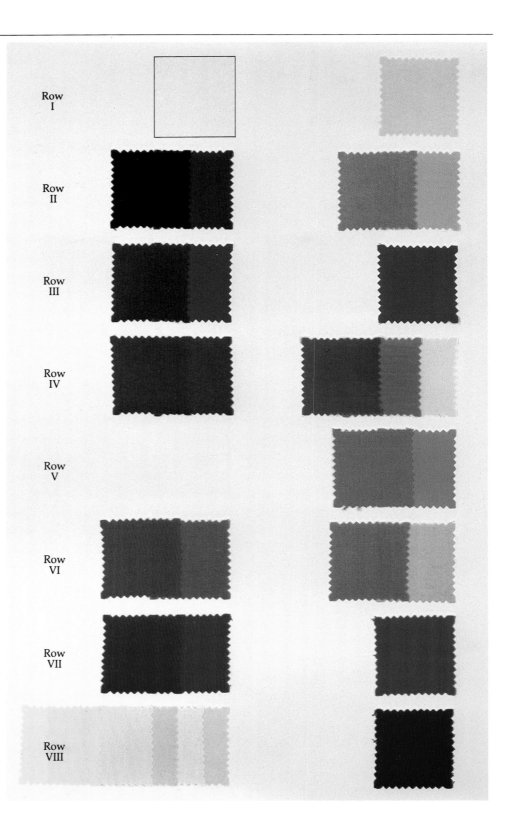

Row I

Row II

Row III

Row IV

Row V

Row VI

Row VII

Row VIII

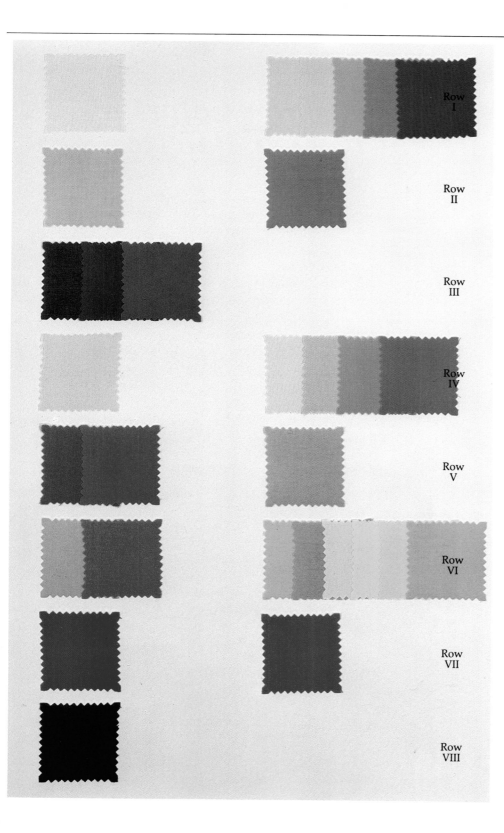

ROW III: The true blues of both seasons are closely related, as are the yellows.

ROW IV: The true greens work in the band, as do all of the true colors.

ROW V: The hot turquoise and Chinese blue of Winter both contain some yellow, and work well with the turquoise of Spring.

ROW VI: The bright warm pinks of Spring are bright enough to be included and the shocking pink and deep hot pink of Winter are true pinks.

ROWS VII & VIII: The true reds and purples of each palette are almost interchangeable.

How to Use Fashion Colors That are not in Your Palette

Each season designers focus on distinctive colors and combinations in their collections. It is possible to successfully wear these fashion colors, even though they may not be in your palette or flow chart. To do so effectively, the color must be worn in combination with a color from your flow chart or in a print that contains one of your flow chart colors. *Most importantly*, this color must be one that will emphasize your most dominant characteristic.

Some colors are favored by the major designers as either fashion colors or classic colors. Fashion colors are likely to change from season to season, while classic colors such as navy blue and gray are available each year. It is easy to combine the classic colors with colors from your flow chart and still be able to wear your correct makeup colors. When wearing a fashion color, care must be taken to use a combination that allows for complementary makeup. Below are suggested color combinations for all types of each season.

Olive

Winters can wear it with *(top row left to right)*
Deep Hot Pink, Magenta, Fuchsia, Hot Turquoise, True Blue, Burgundy, and Blue-Red.

Summers can wear it with *(middle row left to right)*
Soft Fuchsia, Orchid, Periwinkle Blue, and Watermelon.

Springs can wear it with *(bottom row left to right)*
Clear Salmon, Peach, Emerald Turquoise, Light Warm Aqua, Light True Blue, and Bright Golden Yellow.

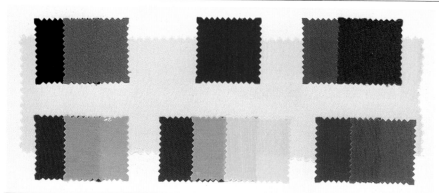

Beige

Winters can wear it with (*top row left to right*)
Black, True Red, Royal Blue, Fuchsia, and Royal Purple.

Summers can wear it with (*bottom row left to right*)
Plum, Mauve, Burgundy, Rose Pink, Pastel Pink, Medium Blue, and Deep Rose.

Peach

Winters can wear it with (*top row left to right*)
Burgundy, Magenta, Deep Hot Pink, and True Red.

Summers can wear it with (*bottom row left to right*)
Rose Pink, Mauve, Deep Rose, and Watermelon.

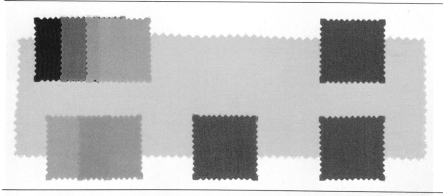

Camel

Winters can wear it with (*top row left to right*)
Royal Purple, Fuchsia, Burgundy, Pine Green, Black, Charcoal Gray, and Blue-Red.

Summers can wear it with (*bottom row left to right*)
Pastel Pink, Mauve, Burgundy, Charcoal Blue-Gray, Periwinkle, and Watermelon.

Brown

Winters can wear it with (*top row left to right*)
Royal Blue, True Red, White, Light True Gray, Fuchsia, Magenta, and Deep Hot Pink.

Summers can wear it with (*bottom row left to right*)
Periwinkle, Sky Blue, Medium Blue, Mauve, Orchid, and Pastel Aqua.

Pink

Autumns can wear it with (*top row left to right*)
Mahogany, Rust, Peach, and Salmon.

Springs can wear it with (*bottom row left to right*)
Orange-Red, Clear Bright Red, Clear Salmon, and Bright Coral.

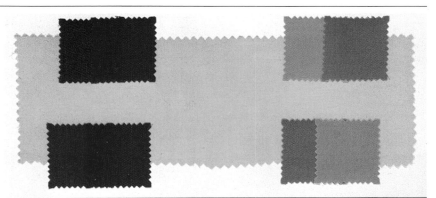

Gray

Autumns can wear it with (*top row left to right*)
Tomato Red, Teal, Salmon, Camel, Gold, and Terra Cotta.

Springs can wear it with (*bottom row left to right*)
Peach, Clear Salmon, Light Warm Aqua, Buff, Clear Bright Red, and Light True Blue.

Burgundy

Autumns can wear it with (*top row left to right*)
Rust, Terra Cotta, Peach, and Tomato Red.

Springs can wear it with (*bottom row left to right*)
Clear Bright Warm Pink, Coral Pink, Light Orange, Clear Salmon, and Orange-Red.

Navy

Autumns can wear it with (*top row left to right*)
Mahogany, Rust, Terra Cotta, Tomato Red, and Gold.

Springs can wear it with (*bottom row left to right*)
Orange-Red, Coral Pink, Bright Yellow-Green, and Bright Golden Yellow.

PART VII
ABOUT COLOR

The Power of Color

Do you dream in black and white or in color? If you dream in color, do you remember your first technicolor dream? Mine occurred when I was seven years old—and I vividly remember it being the flower garden behind my house. Perhaps I remember because I was precocious about color, but it's more likely that I remember because that dream was so beautiful.

We were the first family on the block to have a color television set. So many friends began to "stop in" to watch TV at our house that I toyed with the idea that their visits were a tribute to my popularity. The truth, of course, was that watching television in living color was a hundred times more fun than watching in black and white.

Motion pictures fascinated the public from their earliest beginnings in grainy black and white. But their success skyrocketed with the single new introduction of color. Why was there such a disproportionate increase in these industries when they switched from black and white to color? They literally "came alive" with color, because color has both a dimensional and an emotional affect on each of us. The performers, who had been little more than remote images on our screens in black and white, became real people in color.

Colors have a profound effect on us. As Leatrice Eiseman explains in her book, *Alive With Color* (Acropolis 1983), "Colors evoke emotions—some pleasant, some very unpleasant. You can turn off to a terrific color because of some experience long past." In fact, psychological "color tests" are often given to people who are emotionally disturbed or depressed. Because we have little reason to falsify our responses to color, the technique opens up channels for investigating the problems of those who are unwilling or unable to communicate on a verbal level. Think back to what I said earlier about non-verbal communication; it will help you to recognize that color has its own special prominence, and impact.

If you were to be offered a choice between dressing in the right style or dressing in the right color, which would you choose? Style does have greater importance. But you must understand the *symbiotic effect* of using the best style *and* the best color. Each contributes to your good image, but *together, they more than double the benefits.*

You've analyzed your body type to determine what style of clothing will be best for you. You've gone beyond the visual analysis to incorporate your personality traits, adding another dimension to your wardrobe. The final dimension is that often underestimated but so crucial aspect, color. It's now time to analyze your individual coloring in order to determine your best colors—to add the final dimension to your style.

Why was Carole Jackson's book *Color Me Beautiful* such a runaway success? As I noted earlier, color has a profound psychological affect on all of us. And each of us has that wonderfully human trait called "vanity," which ensures a natural curiosity about which colors are best on us. Finally, Carole was the person who gave us simple and understandable rules about color; about its nature and its proper use as it applies to our unique individual coloring. When introducing any new subject to millions of people, it is important to do so in a simple and logical way so that a strong foundation can be built. When we are first taught math, we are told that it is impossible to subtract five from three. Later, after the negative numbers have been introduced, we are told that we can take five from three and get negative two. This does not mean that the initial information was wrong. It merely indicates the need to continue to build and expand our knowledge to assure success and satisfaction in the future. So let's take the initial information we have received about color, expand upon it, and incorporate your personality so that you will be able to use color to imprint your own vivid individual style.

Q. *I have been in the fashion business for years. I have a natural flair for color and style. Are color and style "rules" really necessary?*

A. Your natural abilities make you one of the lucky ones. Most of us aren't so fortunate. For us, it is important to understand what to look for when selecting clothes so that we can achieve balance and harmony. But even people who have this natural ability find it fun and exciting to understand why what they have been doing works. I bet there are still times when you select something that's not quite right. By understanding the rules, you will be able to "fine-tune" your eye.

Color Characteristics: The Blue and Gold Difference

Before we look at color and how it relates to you personally, it is important to discuss the characteristics of color. We can then form a basis of comparison between colors to see how they are related to each other, and to understand how to use them most effectively. Colors are often divided into different groups as a means of studying their characteristics. One of the most common ways is to separate colors by their basetones. Each color has a blue base or a gold base. Picture the difference between a blue-red and an orange-red or a blue-green and a yellow-green. Since the development of the seasonal color system, it is common to see colors grouped into four separate palettes corresponding to the four seasons of the year. The colors are, however, still related with respect to basetone.

The Winter colors are blue-based; they are bright, clear, vivid, deep, and often described as jewel-like. (Some light, clear icy colors are often included. When used with the deep colors the icy colors increase the depth and contrast of the Winter hues.) The Summer colors are also blue-based, but they are the soft, blended, muted shades often referred to as pastels.

The Autumn colors are gold-based, and are deep, rich, and muted. They are often described as earthy. The Spring colors are also gold-based, but are light, clear, delicate, and considered bright.

Look at the individual palettes—Winter, Summer, Autumn, and Spring—and notice the differences as well as the similarities. The Winter and Summer colors share a blue base while Autumn and Spring are both gold-based. Notice too that the Autumn and Winter colors are deeper and stronger than the Summer and Spring colors.

The Summer and Autumn colors are also related in a more subtle way, as are the Winter and Spring colors. Winter and Spring are bright and clear, Summer and Autumn are softly muted.

The three facets of color

Within each of the palettes there are three clearly identifiable characteristics: the *undertone*, the *intensity*, and the *clarity*. The *undertone* of a color is the basetone, which will be either gold or blue. You will be able to see the difference in virtually all colors; compare blue-green and yellow-green, blue-red and orange-red, and royal blue and teal blue. Some colors are known as true colors. True colors have equal amounts of blue and gold in the base. Compare blue-red, true red, and orange-red and notice the change from blue base to gold base.

The *intensity* of a color refers to how dark or light it is. By adding white to red, you get pink, and by adding black you get maroon. Both pink and maroon are different intensities of red. It is sometimes easier to think of a scale from white to black with ten steps of gray in between. Each step is a different intensity.

The *clarity* of a color is often the most difficult characteristic to see. Its clarity is defined by how bright or soft a color is. To soften a color, gray is added. The effect is a muted color, which is often referred to as "grayed down." There are 14 possible steps in considering clarity of colors at various intensity levels. Some colors are less bright than others. The color red can be made much brighter than the color blue-green. Each color has its own clarity range. The important thing to note is that some colors are bright and others are soft and muted; the *degree* of brightness or softness is not important for our purposes.

In order to clearly see the relationship between all colors, and subsequently their relationship to you, it is easier to look at one characteristic at a time. I will start by considering the relationship between colors that have the same basetone. The Autumn and Spring colors, which have a gold base, are referred to as the "warm" colors. Look at the Autumn-Spring flow chart. The colors are arranged from the deepest and most muted of the Autumn colors to the lightest and clearest of the Spring. There is a gradual movement of each color from one end of the chart to the other. Notice, especially, the colors in the middle band and their similarities.

The "cool" colors of Winter and Summer have a blue basetone. In the Winter-Summer flow chart the colors are arranged from the deepest, brightest, and most vivid of Winter to the lightest and most muted of Summer. The colors in the center band are very closely related. Notice the gradual flow from the dark to the light colors, all with the same basetone.

It is interesting to discover that in both the warm and cool flow charts there is no obvious line of demarcation, where one season stops and the other begins, but rather a gradual movement and flow from one season to the next. As we continue analyzing the other characteristics, the same phenomenon will be seen.

Seeing red about red

I am always amazed when I hear people say with total conviction that they "can't wear red." There are so many shade intensities of red that it is a meaningless statement unless you specify which red. Color expert Albert Munsell, in his study of the characteristics of color, noted that the intensity of a color is its most dominant characteristic—the one that is noticed first. As we continue our study of colors, it is therefore important to look at colors that are related by intensity.

The Winter-Autumn flow chart contains deep, rich colors that are arranged from the brightest and "bluest" of Winter to the most muted and golden of Autumn. Both Autumn and Winter colors are deep in intensity. The colors in the center band of the chart have almost equal amounts of gold and blue and cannot be described as either very golden or very blue. Overall, the Summer-Spring flow chart contains light colors as compared with the Winter-Autumn chart. The colors are arranged from the most blue and muted of Summer to the most golden and clear of Spring. Notice that the colors in the center band are so closely related that some are almost interchangeable.

The final characteristic of color must not be ignored, in spite of the fact that it is less obvious than either the undertone or the intensity. The degree of *clarity* of a color makes a tremendous impact. Consider the difference between a bright vivid magenta and a soft rose. As you add gray to the magenta, you will soften it so that it begins to resemble the soft rose. The current popularity of "neon" colors truly epitomizes the clarity of color.

It is important to compare colors that are related in terms of clarity. The Summer and Autumn palettes both contain muted colors. The Summer/Autumn flow chart colors are arranged from the most blue of Summer to the most golden of Autumn. The center band contains muted colors that are very closely related.

The last flow chart contains bright colors. It is interesting to look at these colors next to the muted ones of Summer and Autumn. The Winter/Spring flow colors have been arranged from the deepest and most blue of Winter, to the lightest and most golden of Spring. Notice the true colors in the center band, which contains colors that are neither too light nor too dark.

It is fascinating to look at the flow charts carefully and to understand that all colors are related to each other in a smooth continuous flow. The intensity, clarity, and basetone of the colors do not change drastically within a season or from one season to another. In addition to the flow from one season to the next, some colors have characteristics that allow them to appear in several flow chart bands. They are the emerald turquoise of Spring, the periwinkle blues, the bright warm pink of Spring, the soft white of Summer, the true gray of Winter, and the soft rose of Summer.

As we worked toward finding the styles that are best for you, we looked at the characteristics of clothing that correspond to the same characteristics of your body, i.e., line and scale. To determine which colors are most complementary to you, we must do the same thing. Now that we have looked at the basetone, intensity, and clarity of colors, we must look at these same characteristics as they apply to your coloring.

Is There a Season for You?

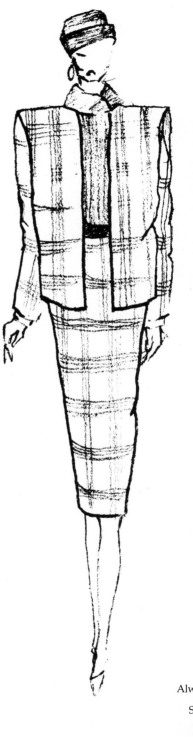

Most of us can remember special colors from the days when we were very young—colors in which we were comfortable and that we enjoyed wearing. Every Easter from as far back as I can remember, my mother dressed my sister and me in navy coats with little white collars, patent-leather Mary Jane shoes, and white Breton sailor hats. I must compliment my mother on her taste and constant dedication to making her daughters look like fashion plates, but I was so relieved when I was finally too old to wear that "Easter" outfit.

I was never very comfortable in that navy coat. The first Easter that I was old enough to pick out my own outfit was so exciting. I chose a beige and cocoa tweed coat, a beige hat, bone shoes, and a bone bag. At the time, I was convinced that I looked and felt so wonderful because I, and not my mother, had selected the outfit. Unfortunately, however, I was not a fast learner. Over the years I realized that although I was always comfortable in browns and beiges, each Spring, because my friends looked so nice in their crisp navy, white, and red outfits, I continued to buy that navy.

Finally, after years of feeling that I looked tired and that I was "coming down with something" every time I wore navy, I decided to give up on it. I began, slowly, to develop a small list of my good and bad colors. It wasn't until five years ago, when I had my first color analysis in London, that I finally understood why certain colors were better on me than others. It suddenly became obvious to me that the colors that had the same characteristics as my coloring would look good on me because they created a balance and harmony when I wore them. These colors were like a natural extension of me and my coloring.

Colors that do not have the same or similar characteristics as my coloring clash and therfore look separate from me. When a color clashes with your coloring, the clash creates shadows, causing lines and wrinkles to show up on your face. A line of demarcation between the color and the person wearing the color is another unhappy result. This is not unlike what happens when you wear clothing that clashes with your body line. It all seemed so simple and logical that I was annoyed at myself for not being able to figure all this out for myself long ago.

The *Color Me Beautiful* concept

Carole Jackson, in her best-selling *Color Me Beautiful*, gave millions of people the opportunity to logically identify colors that are complementary to them. Here's how she describes the relationship between seasonal colors and individual coloring:

Autumn colors are deep, rich, earthy, and muted. The Autumn woman has coloring that is complemented by the golden undertones of the colors of the leaves on the trees, seen on a crisp Autumn day. Spring colors are bright, clear, and delicate. The Spring woman has coloring that is complemented by the warm peach and yellow undertones of the colors of the daffodils, crocuses, and the first blade of grass in the Spring season. Winter colors are blue-based, bright, clear, and vivid. The Winter woman sparkles in vivid primary colors and cool colors like the glittering snowflake on a crisp ski slope. Summer colors are soft, dusty, muted, and blended. The Summer woman glows in the pastels and soft colors of the sea and sky on a hazy Summer day.

By identifying a seasonal group of colors that have characteristics similar to yours, you will begin to better understand your coloring. In order to classify your coloring and thus find your "season," it is necessary to look at your skintone, hair, and eye color. It is possible to identify the *undertone, intensity*, and *clarity* of each of these. Winter and Summer women have a blue base to their skintone and eye color. Their hair color will often be an ash tone with few, if any, golden highlights. The younger you are the more highlights you will see in your hair. However, these highlights are not metallic in color but merely a lightening effect similar to the golden highlights resulting from sun exposure. Autumn and Spring women have a gold base to their skintone and eye color. Their hair will have a metallic golden tone. Occasionally their hair will have an ash tone since as we get older our skintone, eyes, and hair all get softer, creating this ash look. The base color—gold or blue of skintone, hair, and eye colors—of each seasonal type is the *undertone*.

Winter and Autumn women have deeper coloring in their eyes, hair, and skintone than Spring and Summer women. The overall intensity of Autumn and Winter is deeper and stronger. Summer and Spring women have a lighter intensity in their coloring. This "lightness" and "darkness" describe the *intensity* of individual color characteristics. Finally, Summer and Autumn women have a soft muted look to their skintone as well as their eye color. Their haircolor blends with the skintone, creating an overall soft and muted look. Winter and Spring women have a clear bright look to their skintone and eye color. The clarity of the eye color often resembles glass. Their haircolor appears bright and results in a contrast look with their skintone. The muted and bright looks describe the *clarity* of the coloring. In sum, these seasons combine as follows:

- Winter and Summer coloring—Blue (cool) undertone
- Autumn and Spring coloring—Golden (warm) undertone

- Winter and Autumn coloring—Deep intensity
- Summer and Spring coloring—Light intensity
- Summer and Autumn coloring—Muted clarity
- Winter and Spring coloring—Bright clarity

In the four years since *Color Me Beautiful* was published, I have worked to further develop the seasonal color system. My initial role in expanding the color theory developed during my involvement with the Oriental people, the Japanese in particular. All the books on color theory stated that the Oriental skintone was essentially the same, the same undertone as well as intensity and clarity. After living in Japan for five years, I knew this was not true. I have studied the Japanese skintone for the last three years and have color-analyzed thousands of volunteers. As anticipated, I confirmed a wide range of differences in the colors of the skintone, hair, and eyes. This study, and training my eye to recognize the differences, had the additional benefit of allowing me to recognize a wider range of skintone colors in Western countries as well, and to better understand the relationships between the seasons. I have thus been able to compile a list of skintone, hair, and eye colors for all races. This list describes the undertone, intensity, and clarity of skintone, hair, and eye colors. Look at the following charts to help you identify your season.

Chart for Caucasians:

	Skin Tone	Hair	Eye Color
Winter: **blue base,** **deep,** **bright**	olive beige white with pink rose-beige charcoal freckles	blue-black dark brown medium brown ash brown salt and pepper gray (white)	black-brown dark brown dark blue hazel gray-blue gray-green
Summer: **blue base,** **light,** **muted**	rose-beige beige light beige very pink	dark brown ash brown platinum blonde ash blonde golden blonde brown with red	blue green gray-blue gray-green aqua hazel soft brown
Autumn: **gold base,** **deep,** **muted**	golden beige copper beige with golden freckles ivory peach	ash blonde charcoal black chestnut red golden brown golden blonde warm gray	dark brown hazel warm green golden brown turquoise amber teal
Spring: **gold base,** **light,** **bright**	golden beige beige with golden freckles ivory peach	dark brown golden brown auburn golden blonde strawberry blonde flaxen blonde warm gray	clear blue clear green aqua blue green amber

Chart for Blacks:

	Skin Tone	Hair	Eye Color
Winter: **blue base,** **deep,** **bright**	blue-black dark brown with olive dark ash brown dark rose brown	blue-black black brown-black dark brown white/silver	black brown-black red-brown brown
Summer: **blue base,** **light,** **muted**	dark brown rose brown gray-brown cocoa brown	black black-brown dark ash brown soft brown	brown-black red-brown gray-brown hazel
Autumn: **gold base,** **deep,** **muted**	dark golden brown mahogany medium golden brown golden brown with golden freckles bronze	black brown-black chestnut brown golden brown warm gray	brown-black golden brown two-tone brown hazel
Spring: **gold base,** **light,** **bright**	medium golden brown caramel light bronze copper light golden brown with warm freckles	black red-brown medium golden brown light golden brown	dark brown warm brown topaz hazel

Chart for Asians:

	Skin Tone	Hair	Eye Color
Winter: **blue base,** **deep,** **bright**	olive taupe beige white with pink white	blue-black black dark brown medium brown white/silver	black black-brown red brown brown
Summer: **blue base,** **light,** **muted**	beige rose-beige white with pink very pink	dark brown (taupe) ash brown soft brown brown with red cast soft white	dark brown rose-brown soft brown gray-brown
Autumn: **gold base,** **deep,** **muted**	beige golden beige copper bronze ivory peach	black dark brown with red light chestnut brown dark brown medium brown	dark brown brown-black deep golden brown hazel two-tone brown
Spring: **gold base,** **light,** **bright**	warm beige ivory peach rosy peach	black (rare) dark warm brown brown with red warm brown	dark brown golden brown topaz hazel

Identifying your best colors

Think back to your childhood and try to remember your favorite colors. Picture that special outfit in which you always felt so wonderful and received so many compliments. As you look at the individual seasonal charts of Winter, Summer, Autumn, and Spring, identify the chart that contains the largest number of colors that you have successfully worn. Most of us have a mental list of at least some of our good colors, even though we may not have known why they were so good.

Next, look at the charts describing skintone, hair, and eye coloring and once again try to identify the one group that best describes your coloring. As you begin to "zero in" on your own coloring and its characteristics you will better understand your success colors. If you are having difficulty determining your best season, do read the *Color Me Beautiful* book, or make an appointment to see a qualified consultant. By identifying a season that you feel describes your coloring, you will become more aware of your coloring and will have a foundation on which to build an expanded system.

Once you have selected the season that you feel best describes your coloring, go back and look at the charts and notice that there are some skintone, hair, and eye colors that appear in several seasons. Just as in the color flow charts, the skintone, hair, and eye colors are arranged in a continual flow within each season and from one season to the next. When you look at the flow from one season to the next on the charts it becomes obvious that there is no definitive breakoff point at which one season stops and the other begins. Look at the pictures of the models and notice the similarities and differences within each season and from one season to the next.

PART VIII
THE EXPANDED COLOR SYSTEM

The Beginning of the Expanded System

Some of you may have had difficulty trying to decide which specific season best describes your coloring. You may have recognized some of your characteristics in two of the seasons, each of which seems to describe your coloring. During my first color analysis, it was determined that I was a Spring. For the first year, I wore many of the Spring colors and loved them, but found that I was not comfortable in the brightest colors of the palette. During my training to become a consultant, it was decided that I actually looked better in the Autumn palette of colors. I knew that my first analysis was not totally wrong since I still loved and felt good in some of the Spring colors. It wasn't until I had discovered the flow of colors from season to season that it became clear to me that I had coloring that was best described as Autumn, but could reach into the Spring palette. As I looked at the skin tone, hair, and eye color charts, I noticed

especially that my hair was really more Spring-like in color, that my eyes are Autumn in color, and my skin tone is described in both season's charts. I saw a little of myself in both seasons. I realized that if I could use colors from another palette successfully, everyone else had this possibility.

Reflecting back to my early search for freedom in the selection of styles, I was anxious to add colors to my Autumn palette. With my mathematical mind's need for order I realized that I would need a logical explanation of how and why I could expand my palette. I therefore went to work on an expanded system for each season. If I could logically, and realistically, expand the system, then there seemingly would be no limit to the colors we all could wear.

Q. *I hate being called a "season" and looking like everyone else from that season. Whatever happened to the idea of developing individuality and creativity in working with color and style?*

A. There are many kinds of groups. Being a member of a group doesn't mean that you're like the others in it, but merely that you have something in common with them. That's why it's important to understand your physical characteristics—the unique body size and shape, facial features, and coloring you were born with. For balance and harmony you must wear styles that complement these characteristics. Once you understand them, you can put your distinctive personality to work to be as creative as you wish. Each member of the group is an individual, with her own guidelines to follow to insure that her clothing complements her special features. Working within these guidelines actually frees you to better express your fashion personality.

Q. *I am a Winter, but I always get compliments when I wear colors from the Autumn palette. How is this possible?*

A. Some Autumn colors are closely related to the Winter palette—the ones that are deep and not particularly golden. They can be handsome additions to your Winter palette and still allow correct coordination of your wardrobe.

Q. *I have been analyzed by two qualified color consultants. I was told by one that I was a Summer and by the other that I was an Autumn. Which am I?*

A. It is possible for you to have some of the characteristics of both seasons. Your coloring is obviously soft and muted, since both Summer and Autumn colors are muted. You will probably look best in the colors from the center band of the muted flow chart. You can then add colors from the season—Summer or Autumn—with which you're most comfortable.

Q. *I'm getting bored with my 30 colors. I would like more individuality in my selection and use of color. What should I do?*

A. There are hundreds of possibilities within your 30 colors, which were given to you as a guide. Any colors that are obviously *related* to these colors will also be in your palette. But now you can add your flow colors to expand this palette even more. If you are ready to be still more creative, you can wear *any* color by learning to use it in combination with your best colors.

Your *"Flow" Colors*

The more I studied the flow charts and the flow of individual coloring, the more obvious it became to me that each of us, in addition to having a season, can reach in the direction of another season.

If I could determine why I am able to wear some of the colors from the Spring palette, I told myself, I was sure that I would have the key to the expanded color system. I realized that the Spring and Autumn palettes were related because of the golden undertone of the colors. It then occurred to me that if I had to describe my own coloring, the first thing that I would say is that I am golden. As a child, dressed in navy blue and white, my skin looked yellow. Because I didn't know anything about color at that stage in my life, I always thought that my skin was just strange, different from anyone else's in my family. My "yellow" skin was emphasized by the blue-based colors I was wearing! Now I recognize that the "yellow" was really the golden undertone that is obvious in my skin, hair, and eyes. As I thought about the characteristics of my coloring—the basetone, intensity, and clarity—I realized that my most dominant color characteristic is my golden undertone. Because I am neither particularly dark nor particularly light, I couldn't attribute an obvious intensity level to my coloring. Despite the fact that my coloring is not bright, the softness of it is not immediately apparent. The clearest aspect of my coloring is its undertone.

After this discovery, I went to the "golden" flow chart. By starting with the Autumn colors and adding colors from the Spring band, I discovered that I had added all those colors that I had successfully worn as a Spring. Now I could logically add them to my Autumn palette. I realized that if, right from the beginning, I had looked at the chart, started at the middle and moved out in the direction of both my coloring and my comfort, I would also have had my new expanded palette.

Thrilled and enthusiastic, I decided to begin testing the new flow charts in my classes and training sessions. They worked every time. Now everyone could not only have a season, but an expanded season as well.

Determining your new range of colors is very simple. All you need to do is look at the three characteristics of your coloring and determine which one is the most dominant. Once this is known, it is simply a matter of looking at the corresponding flow chart and adding colors from the center band.

Remember that there are three characteristics to choose from; the undertone, the intensity, and the clarity of your coloring. As in looking at the color palettes, it is easier to look at one characteristic at a time. Let me show you now how to determine your major characteristics.

When you found your season, you gained an understanding of your coloring. Since each season encompasses the three characteristics, it is important to try to identify the one that is seen when you look at yourself in the mirror.

Some of you will be obviously golden. If your major characteristic is your golden quality, you will never have been noticed for your fair or dramatic coloring. Instead, you may frequently hear comments like, "you have a lot of red in your hair," or "in the sunlight you look like a redhead." You may have golden freckles or eyes on which you are constantly complimented because of their golden starbursts and warm burnished tone. A medium golden-brown color will always look fabulous on you! If the overall impression that you project has a golden glow and a warm undertone, you have determined your major color characteristic to be golden.

Some of you may have an obvious blue base to your skin tone as seen in your rosy or pink complexion. You too will be neither very dark nor very light and your hair will have an ash tone. Once your hair begins to gray, you may frequently be asked if you frost your hair since your hair will have a pearly gray tone. Your eyes will have a similar gray tone to them, regardless of whether they are blue or green. If your eyes are brown, they will be ash or coal brown and your skin tone will be very pink. You will look wonderful in all shades of blue. If your coloring is predominantly "cool," your major characteristic will be your blue-based skin tone.

If you cannot say with certainty that you are either warm or cool, you may have had difficulty determining your major season. You may, in fact, appear to have almost equal amounts of gold and blue base to your coloring. You should then consider the other two possibilities— the intensity and clarity characteristics.

Are you often described as having strong, vivid, or deep coloring? Do people comment on your dark exotic eyes? Have you ever been asked if you dye your hair because it has such a deep rich color? Do you need contrast and depth in our clothing colors to complement your coloring? Since intensity is the first characteristic that is noticed by the human eye, you should find it easy to decide if your major characteristic is the depth of your coloring.

If your coloring is not deep and strong, you may often have been described as fair, light, or even delicate. Your most frequent compliment may be about your beautiful natural blonde hair. You may often get special attention in public places because your coloring is so light and fragile. Your dark-haired friend will usually have to carry her own suitcase in the airport, while several gentlemen offer to carry yours. You will look wonderful in shades of pink, including the warm pinks. Your most dominant characteristic will be your light coloring.

If you are not obviously warm or cool, and if you cannot say with certainty that you are light or dark, your most dominant characteristic will have to do with the clarity of your coloring. The first thing that you may be able to notice about yourself is that you have a very soft, muted look. In this case, your coloring will definitely be in the medium range with respect to intensity. Bright colors will look garish on you and you will find that your best colors are the most grayed ones. People will often comment on the softness of your look. Your most dominant characteristic will be your muted coloring.

Those of you who have been unable to identify your major characteristic so far probably have very bright, clear coloring. You will find that your skin tone is light, whether it is ivory or porcelain. Your hair is dark in comparison with your skin tone and your eyes are clear and bright, like jewels. You will find that you are most comfortable in the true colors and that you come to life in bright colors. Your most frequent compliment will be about your bright look or "porcelain" complexion. Your most dominant characteristic will be your bright coloring.

Selecting the Right Flow Chart

Once you have determined which characteristic of your coloring is the most dominant one, select the right flow chart to determine your best range of colors. The flow charts are simply arranged in the following manner by the three characteristics; undertone, intensity, and clarity.

- Autumn/Spring*—warm undertone
- Winter/Summer—cool undertone
- Winter/Autumn—deep colors
- Summer/Spring—light colors
- Summer/Autumn—muted colors
- Winter/Spring—bright colors

*For more on how to use the Color Charts, pages 122–133, see page 198.

Start with your season, and add colors from the center band of the flow chart that best describes your most dominant characteristic. These colors will be closely related to the colors from your major season. Alternatively, you may start at the center band and move out in the direction that best describes your coloring and in which you feel most comfortable. Your personal likes and dislikes are very important.

Let's now look at the flow charts and the colors in the center bands of each to analyze more closely how they are related and to show you why you will be able to expand your palette.

In the warm chart of Autumn/Spring, the colors are arranged from the deepest and most muted of Autumn to the lightest and clearest of Spring. Look at the colors in the center band. The oyster, beige, and camel of Autumn are very similar to the ivory and tans of Spring. The yellow-gold, terra cotta, and pumpkin of Autumn are light and clear enough not to appear too heavy next to Spring's light clear gold and golden brown. The salmon and peach of Autumn, although more muted than the salmon and peach of Spring, are still light enough to be in the same range. The orange-reds of Autumn and Spring are essentially interchangeable. It is possible to include the bittersweet of Autumn in this center band. The greens included from both palettes are bright and clear. The teals, turquoises, and aquas of each season are as clearly related as the beiges. The periwinkle and purple of Autumn are only slightly deeper than Spring's periwinkle and violet but are clear and light enough to be in the flow range.

In the cool chart of Winter/Summer, the colors are arranged from the deepest and most vivid of Winter to the softest and most muted of Summer. Notice the colors in the center band. The soft white of Summer is the white that can be worn successfully by everyone. The medium grays of Winter and the blue-grays of Summer are in the same range. The charcoal gray of Winter becomes the black of the middle-band colors. The blues in the Winter flow section are the true blue and the navy. However, the navy will not be as deep as it is in the true Winter palette. The periwinkle of Summer is added in spite of the fact that it is lighter than the other band colors because it is clear enough to work well. The greens and yellows are closely related. The medium pinks of Winter and the rose pink of Summer appear to be almost interchangeable. The deep rose of Summer is a little more muted than some of the other band colors but the depth and richness make it right. The burgundies, blue-reds, and raspberry are truly flow colors. The plum, orchid, and fuchsia of Summer are medium to dark in intensity and the clearest of the Summer colors.

In the deep chart of Winter/Autumn, the colors are arranged from the deepest and bluest of Winter to the most muted and golden of Autumn. Look at the center-band colors. Notice that the deep brown of Autumn is very dark, not particularly golden, and works well with black accessories. Black and charcoal are included in the flow band as neutrals. The mahogany is a cross between rust and burgundy and therefore fits appropriately in the band. Because some rusts are clear and contain more red than orange, that rust is included. To oyster and taupe, Summer's soft white can be added. The turquoise and Chinese blue of Winter contain some yellow in the base and are appropriately included. The teal and turquoise of Autumn create a blue-green effect. The periwinkle is blue and clear enough to be worn with the Winter colors. The true greens of Winter and the pine green are obviously similar to the forest green of Autumn. The olive is the most muted but the intensity and the "gray" effect make it work. The true red of Winter has equal amounts of gold and blue and therefore is directly related to the tomato red of Autumn. The purples are almost interchangeable in the intensity comparison.

In the light chart of Summer/Spring, the colors are arranged from the bluest of Summer to the most golden of Spring. Again, observe the center band. The ivory and buff of Spring are yellow-based but clear. The soft white and light lemon yellow are clear and blend well with the Spring palette. The blue-greens of Summer contain yellow and are clear enough to work with the Spring band colors. The pinks of Spring are warm pinks, with a hint of yellow, and therefore look very similar to the true pinks of Summer. The deep rose is the darkest color in the band but has a slight warm tone. The light true red of Spring contains both blue and gold. The watermelon of Summer actually has a touch of coral in it, and is often referred to as Summer's orange. Spring's emerald turquoise is a blue-green and is therefore closely related to the blue-green of Summer. The turquoises included do not have a strong yellow base. Any periwinkle is compatible with both seasons and cannot be omitted. The medium blue of Summer and the light clear navy of Spring are similar and not too dark to be included in the band. The medium true gray of Winter is an excellent color to be added to the center band since it is not too deep and does not contain an excess of blue. It is a wonderful flow color for both seasons.

The same gradual flow from one season to the next, which was obvious in the warm and cool flow charts, is also apparent on the intensity flow charts of Winter/Autumn and Summer/Spring. Once again, there is no definitive line of demarcation.

In the muted chart of Summer/Autumn, the colors are arranged from the bluest of Summer to the most golden of Autumn. Look at the band colors and notice the browns. The Autumn browns are neither too dark nor especially golden. They are very similar to the cocoa and rose-brown of Summer. The soft white and oyster are closely related; the oyster is a little deeper. The mahogany of Autumn is a muted brown-burgundy and works with many colors in the Summer band. As it becomes more soft and muted, it becomes a better flow color. The greens of Autumn are soft, muted, and greyed. They have an almost pastel quality to them. The forest green is a bit dark, but as it is grayed down, it works well as a flow color. The blue-greens of Summer are the yellowest of the Summer colors and work with the many greens of Autumn. The salmon of Autumn has a warm pink tone as does the rose of Summer. The rose pink and the deep rose are soft and muted. The bittersweet of Autumn is muted, not too deep or golden. The watermelon of Summer has a touch of coral to it and works well, as it did in the Summer/Spring chart. The periwinkles are interchangeable as in most of the charts. The teal of Autumn is muted and is blue-green in tone. The more muted it is, the better it will be as a flow color. The turquoises included are muted and not exceptionally golden. It is amazing to see not only the softness of the color in the flow chart, but the similarities in the band colors when comparing something as subtle as degree of clarity.

In the bright chart of Winter/Spring, the colors have been arranged from the deepest and bluest of Winter to the lightest and most golden of Spring. Notice the center-band colors. The ivory and taupe are closely related. Since the ivory is often very golden, substituting the oyster of Autumn or the soft white of Summer are excellent options. The light and medium grays of Winter are true colors, which are not too dark and work beautifully as flow neutrals. The warm gray is clear enough to be included with the grays of Winter. The true blues of both seasons are closely related, as are the yellows. The true greens work in the band, as do all of the true colors. The hot turquoise and Chinese blue of Winter both contain some yellow, and work well with the turquoise of Spring. The bright warm pinks of Spring are bright enough to be included and the shocking pink and deep hot pink of Winter are true pinks. The true reds and purples of each palette are almost interchangeable.

Warm-Band Colors*

- **Autumn**
  Oyster White
  Warm Beige
  Camel
  Yellow-Gold
  Gold
  Pumpkin
  Orange
  Terra Cotta
  Deep Peach/Apricot
  Salmon
  Orange-Red
  Bright Yellow-Green
  Turquoise
  Teal Blue
  Deep Periwinkle Blue
  Purple

- **Spring**
  Ivory
  Buff
  Light Warm Beige
  Camel
  Light Clear Gold
  Golden Tan
  Medium Golden Brown
  Peach
  Apricot
  Light Orange
  Orange-Red
  Bright Yellow-Green
  Light Warm Aqua
  Clear Bright Aqua
  Emerald Turquoise
  Light Periwinkle Blue
  Dark Periwinkle Blue
  Medium Violet

*For more on how to use the Color Charts, pages 122–133, see page 198.

Cool-Band Colors

- **Winter**
  Light True Gray
  True Gray
  Charcoal Gray
  Taupe
  Royal Blue
  Navy
  Light True Green
  Lemon Yellow
  Shocking Pink
  Deep Hot Pink
  Bright Burgundy
  Blue-Red
  Royal Purple

- **Summer**
  Soft White
  Light Blue-Gray
  Charcoal Blue-Gray
  Rose-Beige
  Cocoa
  Periwinkle Blue
  Medium Blue
  Grayed Navy
  Deep Blue-Green
  Light Lemon Yellow
  Deep Rose
  Rose Pink
  Burgundy
  Blue-Red
  Raspberry
  Plum
  Orchid
  Soft Fuchsia

Deep-Band Colors

- **Winter**
  Charcoal Gray
  Black
  Lemon Yellow
  Taupe
  Hot Turquoise
  Chinese Blue
  True Blue
  Light True Green
  True Green
  Pine Green
  True Red
  Royal Purple

- **Autumn**
  Mahogany
  Dark Chocolate Brown
  Rust
  Oyster White
  Turquoise
  Teal Blue
  Deep Periwinkle Blue
  Forest Green
  Olive Green
  Dark Tomato Red
  Purple

Light-Band Colors

- **Summer**
  Soft White
  Light Lemon Yellow
  Medium Blue-Green
  Deep Blue-Green
  Powder Pink
  Rose Pink
  Deep Rose
  Watermelon
  Pastel Aqua
  Periwinkle Blue
  Sky Blue
  Medium Blue
  Light Blue-Gray
  Charcoal Blue-Gray

- **Spring**
  Ivory
  Buff
  Camel
  Warm Pastel Pink
  Coral Pink
  Clear Bright Warm Pink
  Clear Salmon
  Clear Bright Red
  Emerald Turquoise
  Clear Bright Aqua
  Light Periwinkle Blue
  Dark Periwinkle Blue
  Light Clear Navy
  Light Warm Gray

Muted-Band Colors

- **Summer**
  Soft White
  Rose-Beige
  Cocoa
  Rose-Brown
  Light Lemon Yellow
  Medium Blue-Green
  Deep Blue-Green
  Deep Rose
  Rose Pink
  Watermelon
  Periwinkle Blue
  Pastel Aqua
  Gray-Blue

- **Autumn**
  Oyster White
  Coffee Brown
  Mahogany
  Grayed Green
  Jade Green
  Olive Green
  Forest Green
  Salmon
  Bittersweet
  Deep Periwinkle Blue
  Turquoise
  Teal Blue

Bright-Band Colors

- **Winter**
  Taupe
  Light True Gray
  True Gray
  True Blue
  Lemon Yellow
  Light True Green
  True Green
  Hot Turquoise
  Chinese Blue
  Shocking Pink
  Deep Hot Pink
  True Red
  Royal Purple

- **Spring**
  Ivory
  Light Warm Gray
  Light Clear Navy
  Light True Blue
  Dark Periwinkle Blue
  Bright Golden Yellow
  Emerald Turquoise
  Clear Bright Aqua
  Coral Pink
  Clear Bright Warm Pink
  Clear Bright Red
  Medium Violet

Testing your color choices

If you are still having difficulty finding your most dominant characteristics or if you would like to test your selection, you may try some test colors. Since you have already identified your season, you can look at the three flow charts that contain your season. Compare colors from the center band of these charts.

If you are an **Autumn**, to determine or confirm your flow chart, try:

Autumn/Spring	*Autumn/Summer*	*Autumn/Winter*
Bright Yellow-Green	Deep Blue-Green	True Green
Orange-Red	Watermelon	True Red
Medium Golden Brown	Cocoa	Charcoal Gray

Which is best?

If you are a **Spring**, to determine or confirm your flow, try:

Spring/Autumn	Spring/Summer	Spring/Winter
Teal Blue	Medium Blue	True Blue
Orange-Red	Watermelon	True Red
Bright Yellow-Green	Medium Blue-Green	True Green

Which is best?

If you are a **Summer**, to determine or confirm your flow try:

Summer/Winter	Summer/Autumn	Summer/Spring
Deep Hot Pink	Salmon	Warm Pink
Light True Green	Grayed Green	Emerald Turquoise
Royal Blue	Teal Blue	Light Clear Navy

Which is best?

If you are a **Winter**, to determine or confirm your flow, try:

Winter/Autumn	Winter/Summer	Winter/Spring
Teal Blue	Medium Blue	Light True Blue
Dark Tomato Red	Blue- Red	Clear Bright Red
Forest Green	Deep Blue-Green	Emerald Turquoise

Which is best?

One of the three sets of flow colors will look better on you than the others. These colors and their flow chart will confirm your flow season.

A Different
Notation

Since so many people are familiar with the seasonal system, it may be helpful to consider the following notation:

- As a Winter you will either lean toward
  Summer, Autumn, or Spring: W → S, W → A, W → Sp.

- As a Summer you will either lean toward
  Winter, Spring, or Autumn: S → W, S → Sp, S → A.

- As an Autumn you will either lean toward
  Spring, Winter, or Summer: A → Sp, A → W, A → S.

- As a Spring you will either lean toward
  Autumn, Summer, or Winter: Sp → A, Sp → S, Sp → W.

In each case you start with a major seasonal palette and add a direction into the second season that most closely resembles the dominant characteristics of your coloring. If you have already had your major season confirmed, it is now only necessary to find your direction in order to expand your color palettes. If you have not yet determined your major color season, you may select only a flow chart. You will be able to have your expanded palette immediately. Each of you will have your own "comfort zone."

Some people will find that they are better in the center bands of the flow chart than in a single season. Their unique coloring is a combination of characteristics from two seasons. They will be able to work with the center band colors and reach in the direction in which they are most comfortable.

It is sometimes helpful to look at the individual palettes arranged in a circle with each quadrant containing a season. Thus far we have considered only the individual quadrants of Winter, Summer, Autumn, and Spring.

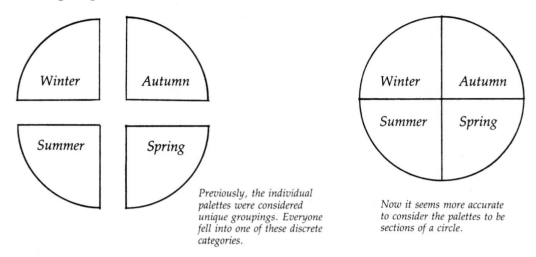

Previously, the individual palettes were considered unique groupings. Everyone fell into one of these discrete categories.

Now it seems more accurate to consider the palettes to be sections of a circle.

Instead of looking at the entire quadrant, look at a *position* on the circle. A circle contains an infinite number of points and each of us has a special point on the circle. By understanding your position you can see your direction and determine your flow season.

As an Autumn, your position can be in the direction of Winter, Summer, or Spring:

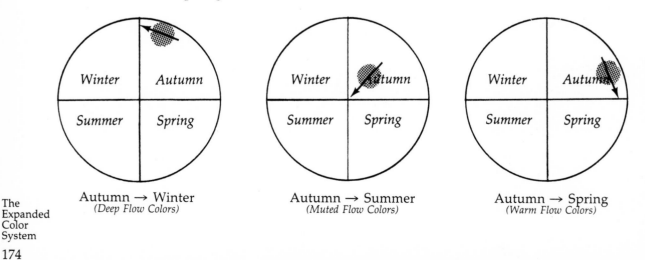

Autumn → Winter
(Deep Flow Colors)

Autumn → Summer
(Muted Flow Colors)

Autumn → Spring
(Warm Flow Colors)

As a Spring your position can be in the direction of Autumn, Summer, or Winter:

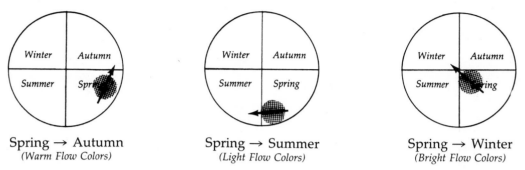

Spring → Autumn
(Warm Flow Colors)

Spring → Summer
(Light Flow Colors)

Spring → Winter
(Bright Flow Colors)

As a Winter your position can be in the direction of Autumn, Summer, or Spring:

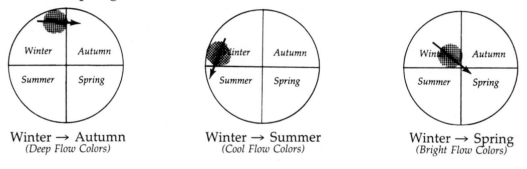

Winter → Autumn
(Deep Flow Colors)

Winter → Summer
(Cool Flow Colors)

Winter → Spring
(Bright Flow Colors)

As a Summer your position can be in the direction of Spring, Winter, or Autumn:

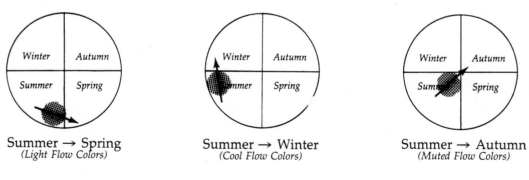

Summer → Spring
(Light Flow Colors)

Summer → Winter
(Cool Flow Colors)

Summer → Autumn
(Muted Flow Colors)

Colors and Your Preferences

Now that we have studied colors and their relationship to your physical coloring, let's consider your personality and the psychological affects that color can have on you. Social scientists, in studying the negative and positive effects that colors have on many people, have discovered some fascinating reactions to color.

Birren, in his book *Color in Your World*, associated the color red with feelings of excitement, power, and stimulation on the positive side, and feelings of aggression, defiance, or competitiveness on the negative. In either case, the color red evokes strong feelings. Earlier I mentioned that the comment, "I can't wear red" tends to be a meaningless statement, considering the many shades and intensities of the color. However, to say "I can't wear red" can become *very* meaningful if you are referring to your personal preferences and the psychological affect that the color red has on you. *You should never wear a color about which you feel negative.*

Al Hackl, President of Colortone Press and Acropolis Books Ltd., has also studied the psychological affects of color in terms of its use in printing to attract attention, improve legibility, and enhance appeal. It can be extremely helpful to understand why you have the feelings that you do about certain colors. On the following page is a list of some colors and the positive and negative reactions they produce.

Psychological Effects of Color

Color	Positive Feelings	Negative Feelings
Yellow	Sunny Cheerful Optimistic	Egocentric Dishonest Sensational
Cream	Tranquil Quiet Consoling Comfortable Natural	Commonplace Invokes envy Immature
Blue	Serene Calm Comfortable Cool Secure	Depressing Melancholic
Violet	Regal Dignified	Cruel Pompous
Brown	Dependable Realistic	Boring Obstinate
Pink	Soft, calm Sweet Tender	Effeminate
White	Pure Innocent Spiritual	Sterile
Gray	Secure Peaceful Protective	Dreary Colorless
Black	Sophisticated	Empty Deathly
Green	Natural Youthful Peaceful	Envy Immaturity

Each flow chart contains a full range of colors with respect to intensity and clarity. Therefore, you are free to select only those colors that are pleasing to you and eliminate any that you feel negative about.

Some of you are conservative and will be content with the selection of colors from your seasonal palette. After all, they are your best colors and you know how well you look in them. Your 30 colors are guides, and if you peek between these guides, you know that there are really hundreds of colors for you.

Others of you are ready now to expand into your flow charts. These colors will allow you to expand your range of colors and still look fabulous. Begin slowly adding colors from the center band. You will love the flexibility you now have in creating your expanded wardrobe.

The Outraged Woman

After each and every one of my color lectures during the past few years, there has always been one woman who objected violently to being limited to a single palette of colors. She often bordered on real hostility; mentally stamping her foot, she would defiantly assert, "I WILL WEAR ANY COLOR I WANT TO WEAR!" In retrospect, she was often the one person in the audience who always caught my eye because she made such a strong non-verbal impact through her fashion statement.

In the beginning we learned which lines, scales, prints, and textures of clothing are correct for our body type by looking at our face shape and body shape. Upon consideration of our personality, we expanded on this information to create a wardrobe that projects each of us as individuals. Just as we "added to" or "multiplied" information to attain our style, so should we determine our direction with colors to *complete* our style.

Our "outraged" woman wants to wear any—and every—color. She understands, perhaps, that some colors look better on her than others, but does not want to be limited to a palette, or to a flow chart. She feels that she is justified, through her strong desire and conviction, to wear any color, especially the fashion colors. Let's look at how she *can* wear her "fashion" colors and still look fabulous.

This Season's Fashion Colors: How to Wear Them Successfully

In order to wear the fashion colors that are not in your palette or flow chart, you must first accept the fact that colors that are neither in your palette nor in your flow chart will clash with your coloring and will not be complementary when worn as a single color. Yet it is possible to use these colors to create the balance and harmony for which we have been striving. To do so effectively, the color must be worn in a print or in combination with a color from your flow chart. MOST IMPORTANTLY, this color from the flow chart must be one that will emphasize your most dominant color characteristic.

If you are "golden" you must select one of the "most golden" colors as your emphasis so that the total effect created will still complement your coloring. As a golden Autumn, I am now able to wear my favorite color, royal blue. I wear it with gold, warm beige, terra cotta, and the warm greens. I do not wear it with my reds, purple, periwinkle, or coffee brown. By using my flow colors as well as my seasonal colors, my possible "golden" combinations are increased.

Some colors are favored by the major designers as either fashion colors or classic colors. Fashion colors are likely to change from season to season, while classic colors such as navy blue and gray are available every year. Let's look at some of these colors and see how everyone can wear them.

Moss and olive green are used frequently by designers. They are gold-based colors from the Autumn palette. Moss green used alone by any Winter will not be complementary. Burgundy, fuchsia, magenta, hot pink, red, true blue, and turquoise all look fabulous with moss green. These colors include possibilities for a contrast look for all types of Winters, depending on the intensity of their coloring. In each case, the moss will be used away from the face and the color from the flow chart will be used as the major statement of the outfit.

A Summer strives for a soft, muted, and blended look. How soft and muted will depend on the individual and her most dominant color characteristic. Many colors from the Summer palette will work well with moss green. Soft fuchsia, orchid, mauve, watermelon, periwinkle blue, and soft burgundy are all good choices.

Since moss is an Autumn color, the entire Autumn palette works well with it. Yet all Autumns cannot wear it effectively. Those who need contrast for their best look will wear it away from the face or with tomato red, mahogany, rust, or the true red of Winter. Those who need a soft muted look will wear it with oyster, beige, or one of the softer greens. Once again, we are striving for a balance and harmony with your coloring.

The Spring who wants to wear moss green should choose the brightest colors from her palette to achieve a look of contrast and clarity. Possible colors to combine with moss are bright coral, bright golden yellow, warm peach, clear bright aqua, light true blue, and emerald turquoise.

There are thousands of possible combinations with moss green and other fashion colors that will allow you to be creative, individual, and still look fabulous.

Special Combinations of Colors from each Palette With the Fashion Colors

	Winter	Summer	Autumn	Spring
Camel	Burgundy Black Royal Purple Blue-Red Charcoal Fuchsia Pine Green	Soft Burgundy Mauve Charcoal Blue-Gray Pastel Pink Periwinkle Watermelon	All Colors	All Colors
Beige	Black True Red Royal Blue Royal Purple Fuchsia	Medium Blue Rose pink Mauve Soft Burgundy Plum Deep Rose Pastel Pink	All Colors	All Colors
Dark Brown	Light True Gray Magenta Deep Hot Pink True Red White Royal Blue Fuchsia	Periwinkle Orchid Mauve Sky Blue Medium Blue	All Colors	Peach Light Bright Aqua Salmon Orange-Red Bright Golden Yellow
Peach	True Red Deep Hot Pink Burgundy Shocking Pink	Rose Pink Deep Rose Mauve Watermelon	Moss Teal Blue Brown Bronze	All Colors

Chart continues on the next page.

Special Combinations of Colors from each Palette with the Fashion Colors (*continued*)

	Winter	Summer	Autumn	Spring
Rust	Burgundy Blue-Red Fuchsia	Pink Blue-Red	All Colors	Light True Blue Turquoise Aqua Peach
Mustard	Burgundy True Red Fuchsia	Soft Burgundy Rose	All Colors	Light True Blue Orange-Red
Fuchsia	All Colors	Soft Pink Mauve Blue-Gray	Rust Terra Cotta	Peach Coral
Gray	All Colors	All Colors	Tomato Red Terra Cotta Camel Salmon Gold Teal Blue	Peach Clear Salmon Orange-Red Lt. Warm Aqua Lt. True Blue Buff
Burgundy	All Colors	All Colors	Rust Terra Cotta Deep Peach Tomato Red	Lt. Orange Clear Bright Warm Pink Clear Salmon Coral Pink Orange-Red
Navy	All Colors	All Colors	Tomato Red Terra Cotta Gold Rust Mahogany	Orange-Red Coral Pink Bright Golden Yellow Bright Yellow-Green

	Winter	Summer	Autumn	Spring
Pink	All Colors	All Colors	Rust	Clear Salmon
			Mahogany	Bright Coral
			Salmon	Clear Bright Red
			Deep Peach	Orange-Red

Many of these fashion colors are neutrals. It is easier to use them with colors from the palettes that allow for coordination of the wardrobe and use of proper and complementary makeup. Other colors, including pink, peach, and perhaps some of your favorites, will also work. However, it takes a little more confidence and daring to try the unusual combinations. The results can be fantastic, but only you will know when you are ready to give them a try.

Notice that the list of special color combinations includes all types of each season. With camel, for example, the pine green, true red, royal purple, and black will work well for the Winter/Autumn flow individual. The blue-red, burgundy, charcoal gray, and fuchsia will work for those who are Winter/Summer, and the true red will work for those who are Winter/Spring.

The biggest and most frequently asked question is "What about black?" Most women grow up thinking that black is the most basic, most professional, and most sophisticated color that a woman can wear. With the introduction of seasonal analysis, black has become the most controversial of all colors, since it appears only in the Winter palette. Surprisingly, not even all Winters can wear black successfully as a single color next to their face, as it is the strongest of all colors. But wearing black successfully is now possible for all women who know the rules and limitations, as long as they have the desire and personality to wear it with confidence. Simply be certain that it is worn away from the face or in combination with one of your best colors. Remember that the intensity of your makeup should be heightened if you choose to wear it as a single color.

You CAN Wear All Colors

Thus far, our discussion of color has been based on the assumption that we are looking for colors that are naturally in balance and harmony with our coloring. Yet depending on your personality and the occasion, an unusual effect may sometimes be desired. At these times, balance and harmony may not be your goals.

A Winter with contrast to her coloring may want to soften her overall appearance—perhaps for a romantic evening at home! She can do this by adding a softer color not found in her palette. The Summer with soft muted coloring may tire of the softness and want to wear bright colors for a fun change. She can use the bright colors to create the excitement she's seeking.

In extreme cases, as evidenced by the "punk" look, you may choose to wear a single color that is not related at all to your coloring. The person who is most likely to wear non-complementary colors and styles likes to be noticed and wants the freedom to be able to "go for it." She has the personality, physical characteristics, and self-understanding to wear the outrageous and to enjoy the look. She now has the knowledge to successfully create her most outrageous look.

On the following page are some useful guidelines for expanding your use of colors. It is always important to start with your seasonal colors. You can then add colors as you are ready, depending on your personality and needs. You'll find many fascinating steps along the way as you slowly add additional colors.

Guidelines For Expanding Color Use

- *Single seasonal palette*

  Important to understand single seasonal palette, learn to appreciate balance and harmony, become adept at recognizing and working with your best colors.

- *Seasonal palette and flow colors*

  Add flow colors once you have worked with and understand seasonal colors. Everyone should strive to add flow colors in due time.

- *Seasonal palette, flow colors, and use of fashion colors*

  Once flow colors are used successfully and comfortably, add fashion colors. Those who prefer a high-fashion look will be eager to begin to wear these colors. Those who are more conservative may decide to work only with flow colors.

- *Use of all colors*

  Those who want an extreme look may choose to use all colors, regardless of balance and harmony with their coloring, to make a predetermined statement.

Are Your Colors Dramatic, Natural, Elegant, or Delicate?

Certain words used in the fashion world, some of which I have already defined in terms of style, may also be defined in terms of colors. You are now ready to create any look you want since you have an understanding of all the elements of style. You may use these definitions as your final input in your study.

- *Dramatic Colors* are bright, vivid, deep, and provide a lot of contrast.
- *Elegant Colors* are rich, deep, muted, and have little contrast.
- *Rich Colors* are deep, intense, and strong.
- *Delicate Colors* are light, bright, and clear.
- *Vibrant Colors* are vivid, bright, and clear.
- *Pastel Colors* are light and soft.
- *Sharp Colors* are deep and clear. A sharp line or picture has clarity and contrast.
- *Matte Colors* are soft and muted.
- *Natural Colors* are deep, rich, and earthy.
- *Classic Colors* are neutral.
- *Romantic Colors* are any colors that create the mood for your own definition of romantic.

Grand Finale or Just the Beginning?

Following the tremendous success and popularity of color analysis in recent years, some people have been concerned about looking like part of a group. I began to notice that instead of compliments about how wonderful I looked in my colors, I was hearing comments like "you must be an Autumn."

Now all this has changed. Not since the early days of teaching those first color classes have I felt such excitement. The compliments are once again, "how wonderful you look!"—not just how great I look in my colors. The difference: being able to look fabulous *by expressing who you are* in a correct, and thus complementary, way.

All of my original color clients are coming back into class to learn which flow chart is theirs; which one will help them to successfully expand their colors. Those who have the desire to reach further are learning ways to wear all colors, how to coordinate their new colors with their existing wardrobes, and how to create stunning, unique looks in order to satisfy their individual needs. Each one now has her own personal style—her own line, scale, and colors.

Let's take a final moment to reflect on the categories of style. Classic generally describes a formal, conservative style of dressing. Natural describes a less formal, more relaxed, casual style. Romantic describes a dressy, yet formal style. Dramatic describes an exaggeration of one of the three, whether it be formal, casual, or dressy.

Now that you understand the times, places, and occasions when each style is appropriate—and understand your body line and personality—you know in which category (or categories) you are most comfortable. You're now ready to use this knowledge to expand your horizons. Only you know who you are, and who you want to become. I hope I have helped you span that bridge, regardless of its height and length, to be *Always in Style*.

Index

How to use the Color Charts

Season A

This is a complete palette of one season's colors.

Season B

This is a complete palette of one season's colors.

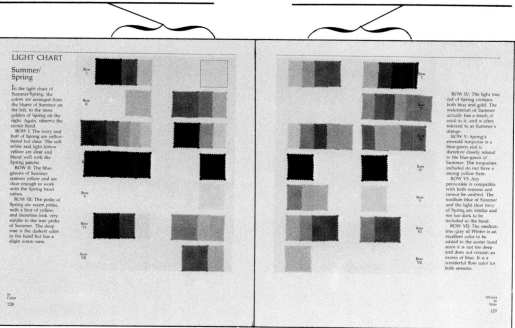

Non-flow Colors

These are colors *not* related to the other season in this chart.

Flow Colors

These are the colors most related to the other season in this chart. These are the centerband colors discussed in the text.

Flow Colors

These are the colors most related to the other season in this chart. These are the centerband colors discussed in the text.

Non-flow Colors

These are colors *not* related to the other season in this chart.

198

Always In Style with *Color Me Beautiful* ORDER CARD

☐ *Always in Style* **Fashion Portfolio ($25.00)—**
A handsome portfolio folder available twice a year, Fall/Winter and Spring/Summer, containing:

1. a 24-page book of the fashion trends including fabrics, colors, accessories, and original fashion drawings to keep you abreast of the fashion trends.
2. a 12-page booklet that pictures those fashions and accessories that complement your body line; straight, soft-straight, or curved.
3. a full-color sheet on the fashion colors for the season.
4. a full-color sheet on fabrics and prints for the season.
5. a sheet of wardrobe silhouette drawings for your body line.

☐ Please send me the newest Portfolio for $25.00
☐ Please send me the next two Portfolios for $40.00

My body type is ☐ Straight ☐ Soft-Straight ☐ Curved

☐ *Color Me Beautiful* **swatches ($20.00)—**
(contains 30 fabric swatches, 10-window clear vinyl holder, white wallet, and makeup guide) Check your season:

My season is ☐ Winter ☐ Summer ☐ Autumn ☐ Winter

☐ *Always In Style* **flow colors ($7.50)—** (contains flow swatches and a 6-window vinyl holder designed to fit your existing wallet holder) Check your flow season:

☐ Autumn→Spring   ☐ Winter→Summer
☐ Autumn→Winter   ☐ Winter→Autumn
☐ Autumn→Summer   ☐ Winter→Spring
☐ Spring→Autumn   ☐ Summer→Winter
☐ Spring→Summer   ☐ Summer→Spring
☐ Spring→Winter   ☐ Summer→Autumn

☐ **More Information.** Please send me more information about *Always In Style*

Please fill out this coupon and mail with your check or money order *payable to Accolade, Inc.,* to the following address:
        Always In Style   c/o Accolade, Inc.
        P.O. Box 3275, Lynchburg, VA 24503

Please send my order to:

Name_____

Address_____

_____Zip_____

If you would like the name of the *Color Me Beautiful/Color For Men* Consultant nearest you, or information on how to become a *Color Me Beautiful* Consultant, call:
        U.S. 800-533-5503   In VA 800-572-2335   In Canada 1-800-633-1010
or write to the following address: Carole Jackson, P.O. Box 3241, Falls Church, VA 22043

If you want information on *CAROLE JACKSON Cosmetics,* call or write the address above.

Exclusive Gift Offer